PASTOR SEARCH
COMMITTEE HANDBOOK

LifeWay Press®
Nashville, Tennessee

ISBN 978-1-4158-5214-9 • Item 005035459

Dewey decimal classification: 254
Subject heading: PASTOR SEARCH COMMITTEE

Scripture quotations are taken from the Holman Christian Standard Bible®, copyright © 1999, 2000, 2002, 2003, 2009 by Holman Bible Publishers. Used by permission. Holman Christian Standard Bible®, Holman CSB®, and HCSB® are federally registered trademarks of Holman Bible Publishers.

Much of the information and many of the tools in this handbook are adapted from approaches and resources used by Baptist state-convention leaders who regularly work with pastor-search committees. These leaders graciously gave permission to include their material in this resource without footnotes. Four of these leaders—Clyde Cain (Oklahoma), Leonard Dupree (Georgia), Sylvan Knobloch (Illinois), and Wayne Oakes (North Carolina)—worked on a writing team led by Robert Sheffield of LifeWay Christian Resources. Ernest Mosley, retired executive vice president, Southern Baptist Convention Executive Committee, and Henry Webb, retired director of Pastoral Ministries at LifeWay Christian Resources, provided key work in bringing this resource to completion. We gratefully acknowledge the work of all contributors.

To order additional copies of this resource, write to LifeWay Resources Customer Service; One LifeWay Plaza; Nashville, TN 37234; fax 615-251-5933; email orderentry@lifeway.com; phone toll free 800-458-2772; or order online at LifeWay.com.

Printed in the United States of America

Groups Ministry Publishing • LifeWay Resources
One LifeWay Plaza • Nashville, TN 37234

Contents

Phase 3: How Do We Let God Lead Us to the Right Pastor?

Phase 4: How Should We Present the Prospective Pastor?

Phase 5: How Do We Give the Pastor a Good Start?

- Pastor-Church Relations Team
- Orientation to the Community
- Annual Performance Review
- Pastor-Appreciation Day

Toolbox

The following tools are provided on pages 43–94 and online
at *www.lifeway.com/pastorsearchcommitteehandbook.*

1. Pastor Search Committee Retreat
2. Directory of Baptist State Conventions
3. Pastor Search Committee Covenant of Agreements
4. Pastor-Church Covenant of Relationship
5. Pastor's Salary, Housing, Benefits, and Expenses
6. Checklist for Pastor's Salary, Housing, Benefits, and Expenses
7. Pastor Search Congregational Survey
8. Position Insights and Leading from Your Strengths Profiles
9. Demographic Profile of Church Membership
10. Directory of Southern Baptist Seminaries
11. Biographical Profile
12. Prospective-Pastor Evaluation
13. Degrees Related to Pastoral Ministry
14. Confidential Personnel Information
15. Reference Release
16. Portfolio of Church and Community
17. Letter for Written References
18. Character-Reference Inquiry
19. Letter for Telephone Interviews
20. Interview Questions
21. Sermon Evaluation
22. Credit and Legal Information Release
23. Request for Criminal-Records Check and Authorization
24. Letter to Prospective Pastor About Questionnaire
25. Prospective-Pastor Questionnaire
26. Service of Installation and Commitment
27. Installation Service
28. Pastor-Church Relations Team
29. Performance Review

Introduction

Pastor Search Committee Handbook is designed to be practical in content, user-friendly in approach, and comprehensive in scope. It addresses the needs of churches of various sizes and is simple enough that all churches will find it easy to use. Although the process is detailed, it is not cumbersome.

The first question a church without a pastor should ask is, Who can give us the leadership we need in this time of transition? Perhaps adequate leadership can be provided by a staff member or by other church members. Or maybe the church should call a transitional pastor to help the church thoroughly prepare to call a new pastor. Optional approaches to this transitional period are described in phase 1.

One role a transitional pastor may fill is serving as a consultant to the pastor search committee. If your church has already elected a committee, it may be best to delay its search activities until the church, with the assistance of a transitional pastor, has completed the important stages of preparation for calling a new pastor. If the church elects a pastor search committee first and then decides to call a transitional pastor, the committee may study the church constitution and bylaws for information about what the church desires of the search committee and the process it will follow when it begins its work. Careful study of these documents will save valuable time and will prevent duplicating efforts as the committee carries out its assignment.

If the committee perceives that the constitution, bylaws, or other policies and procedures need to be changed, recommendations should be taken to the church for approval. The church should officially change a policy that prescribes a procedure before a committee unilaterally changes the procedure. The committee must remember that its purpose is to help the church find the man God calls to serve as its pastor. In Baptist church polity the ultimate decision-making authority lies with the church, under the guidance of the Holy Spirit.

The search committee should spend much time in prayer seeking God's guidance. Only the Holy Spirit can perfectly guide the committee in finding God's man to lead God's church. Human reasoning is never adequate for spiritual challenges. Regular, frequent sessions of corporate prayer can prepare the committee to begin its work and can keep it in the right spirit and on the right course to find the right pastor.

Pastor Search Committee Handbook recommends a five-phase process in calling a pastor:

Phase 1: Our Pastor Has Resigned! What Do We Do Next?

Phase 1 provides information about the transitional process and the selection and organization of the pastor search committee.

Phase 2: How Do We Gather the Information We Need?

This section provides a process of information gathering, a critical part of the search.

Phase 3: How Do We Let God Lead Us to the Right Pastor?

This phase contains information about the actual selection process that gets you ready to present the prospective pastor to your church for consideration.

Phase 4: How Should We Present the Prospective Pastor?

Phase 4 is a presentation/recommendation process that involves the church in affirming the committee's search for the pastor God has prepared for your church.

Phase 5: How Do We Give the Pastor a Good Start?

This section provides guidance for giving a new pastor and his family a good beginning. Remember that you and your pastor will have only one opportunity to have a right start.

The toolbox in this handbook (pp. 43–94) provides useful forms, sample letters, and other tools that will help the committee carry out its responsibilities. All of these items are also provided in PDF and RTF formats for download at *www.lifeway.com/pastorsearchcommitteehandbook*. Delete the tool numbers and reproduce the forms you need or modify the forms to fit your circumstances. You have permission to modify, print, and duplicate these tools to meet the needs of your church.

A word of caution is in order before turning to phase 1: in the past the way a man preached was the determining factor in calling a pastor. That's why the search committee was usually called a pulpit committee. Today a pastor search committee must evaluate preaching skill but must also give careful attention to leadership and personal-ministry skills. The prince in the pulpit often fails if he is a pauper in interpersonal relationships, which are crucial to leadership and personal ministry. In pastor-church relations a good match is a wonderful thing. The church is blessed, and God is honored.

This handbook uses the terms *candidate(s)*, *prospects(s)*, and *prospective pastor(s)* to refer to the same person or persons. Pastor search committees may use one term of their choice or all of these terms interchangeably.

Profile, meaning *a precise biographical sketch*, is used instead of *résumé*. You may use the term with which you are most comfortable. The officer term *chairman* is used without regard to gender.

As you read the material in this handbook and progress through the phases of your search, remember that speed is not the priority; finding and doing the will of God is.

Phase 1

Our Pastor Has Resigned! What Do We Do Next?

Understanding the Transitional Period in the Life of a Church

Many church members see the period between pastors as the "hold things together and keep things going" period. Nominal church members likely view it as the "wait and see" period. Church members who attend only Sunday-morning services may use it as the "I'll just stay home since my preacher left us" period. Prospective church members often treat it as the "a bird in the hand is worth two in the bush; look elsewhere" period. But with effective transitional leadership, the period between pastors can be very productive—a time of growth in personal and congregational worship, evangelism, fellowship, discipleship, and personal and family ministries. Churches passing from the leadership of one pastor to another may be well served by transitional pastors who help make the passage as positive and constructive as possible, gaining momentum and productivity in the process of change.

Some churches without pastors have smooth transitions because of the healthy ministry of the former pastor and a cadre of effective ministry leaders in the church. Even these churches need help in dealing with grief resulting from the loss of a helpful and trusted friend, in overcoming fear that accompanies the uncertainties of change, and in developing trust in a new pastor who has a personality and style that differ from those of the former pastor. Other churches have rough transitions because the previous pastor left just before relationships and trust were damaged beyond repair. Some churches have crisis transitions because of the circumstances surrounding the previous pastor's departure and because of a variety of disabilities that render church leaders spiritually unprepared to guide the church through emotional healing and comprehensive preparation for a new pastor.

Considering Pastoral-Leadership Options for Periods Without a Pastor

Most churches choose from the following options to provide pastoral leadership during the time between pastors.

1. The church may call a transitional pastor to lead ongoing church ministries and to guide the church through the situational and psychological stages of transition that end in employing and engaging with a new pastor.
2. Multiple-staff churches may assign pastoral responsibilities to staff members according to their gifts and available time.
3. Preachers may be enlisted to preach in one or more services, giving church members opportunities to hear a variety of preachers during this period.
4. A preacher may be employed to preach in some or all meetings of the congregation in which sermons are appropriate. In such arrangements other pastoral duties may be assigned to church-staff members or to lay leaders.
5. A person may be employed to provide limited pastoral-ministry services according to his availability.

Many churches without pastors need transitional pastors with experience, training, and ministry gifts that ensure high-quality transitional leadership. Transitional pastors are prepared to lead churches through smooth transitions, rough transitions, and crisis transitions. They may serve effectively as a preacher, a pastor, and a consultant.

LifeWay Christian Resources assists churches by enlisting, training, and providing resources for transitional pastors to serve during the period between pastors. Its aim is to meet the following objectives, which focus on church health and which result in church growth and kingdom priorities.

1. Churches will become more effective as they learn from past experiences, free themselves from hindering traditions, replace discord with harmony, and plan ministries strategically instead of traditionally.
2. Churches will develop more effective church practices.
3. Churches experiencing decline or a growth plateau will experience spiritual and numerical growth. Growing churches will accelerate.
4. Churches will grow in their understanding of pastoral ministry and in their appreciation of pastors and their families.
5. More members will become personally involved in their churches' ministries.
6. Energy previously spent addressing conflict will be redirected to expanded ministries.
7. The next pastor's tenure will be increased, sparing the church the expense of frequent pastoral changes and making more money available for ministries.
8. Thus, the percentage of churches without pastors will decrease. Less time will be spent in interim mode with growth plans put on hold.

Transitional pastors lead churches to move from one pastor to another regardless of the reasons for being without a pastor. They help the church bring closure to one era of pastoral leadership, prepare thoroughly for calling a new pastor, and launch a new pastoral-leadership era. The transitional ministry process involves the following stages.

1. View the church's history through the eyes of Christ.
2. Assess the church's current reality.
3. Affirm biblical principles for church growth.
4. Focus on Kingdom results.
5. Establish church practice.
6. Refocus the church around mission.
7. Find a pastor to lead in fulfilling God's future for the church.
8. Help the pastor make a good start in the church and community.

Churches that choose to use a transitional pastor will include the pastor search committee on the transitional focus team led by the transitional pastor. The search committee will have the benefit of the transitional pastor's counsel in the processes to be followed, a more focused church to serve, and many valuable information resources for use in the search.

For more information about transitional-pastor ministry, contact Pastoral Ministries; LifeWay Christian Resources; One LifeWay Plaza; Nashville, TN 37234-0157; 615.251.2216. For training opportunities visit *www.lifeway.com/ article/transitional-pastor-overview.* You can also download a video by visiting *YouTube.com* and searching for "Transitional Pastor Ministry."

Selecting the Pastor Search Committee

Now that the church is ready to call a new pastor, at the appropriate time the church will enlist a pastor search committee. Enlistment can be done in several ways. Before beginning the selection process, the church should consult its bylaws to learn the process for finding and calling a pastor. If no guidelines are found, the search committee may recommend appropriate policies and/ or procedures for approval by the church. If existing policies and procedures hinder the committee's work, revisions can be proposed to the church.

Before proceeding, consider some common mistakes churches and pastor search committees make in the process of searching for a new pastor.

1. Forming a pastor search committee that doesn't represent all the church
2. Providing an unclear assignment from the church
3. Providing unclear committee guidelines
4. Failing to keep confidences within the committee
5. Not doing a congregational self-study
6. Working with a poorly organized search process
7. Considering the interim or transitional pastor as a pastoral candidate
8. Having more than one committee member contact prospects
9. Not being honest with candidates about your church situation
10. Not preparing well for interviews
11. Not considering the candidate's family throughout the process

12. Not being discreet when visiting a prospective pastor's church
13. Considering only the pulpit skills of a prospective pastor
14. Considering more than one candidate at a time
15. Not checking all references thoroughly
16. Moving the process too fast, being impatient
17. Communicating poorly or inadequately with pastoral prospects
18. Failing to get all agreements in writing
19. Allowing inadequate time for the prospective pastor and the church to get to know each other
20. Treating the search as a human process instead of a spiritual process[1]

Size of the Committee

If your church bylaws specify the number to serve on a pastor search committee, follow that procedure. For most churches five to seven members should be enough for the committee. Determine the suitable number according to resident membership. Smaller-membership churches should not need more than five members. Larger-membership churches may be served well by seven members. Guard against having too large a committee. When a committee becomes too large, everything about the committee process becomes more complicated than is necessary and helpful. If a church bylaw calls for a very large committee, ask the church to consider revising the bylaw.

Selecting Alternates

Some churches elect alternates to serve in case a regular member becomes ill or resigns. Alternates normally don't have the right to vote, even though they may meet regularly with the committee. However, this approach is not recommended unless a church's bylaws require it. In the unlikely event that a committee member resigns, the church can elect a person at that time. Because the need for alternates does not occur often, it unnecessarily complicates the process of determining the membership of the committee and the present-but-inactive status of alternate members.

Candidates for the Pastor Search Committee

Good candidates for the pastor search committee are characterized by—
1. continuing spiritual growth;
2. spiritual discernment;
3. knowing Bible truths and practicing them;
4. faithful attendance and support of the church;
5. skills as a team player;
6. willingness to maintain confidentiality;
7. freedom to attend meetings and occasionally travel;
8. priority commitment to seeking and doing God's will;
9. absence of a self-serving agenda.

Additionally, members of the search committee should represent all segments of the church. Some churches' documents clearly require that persons from certain age groups serve on the committee. Whether or not that is true of your church, include individuals from different age groups. Regardless of age, persons selected should possess a maturity level that fits the list of qualifications.

In no case should your church ask a person to serve on the committee just to satisfy a faction in the church. The committee needs to consist of persons whom church members are led by the Lord to select and persons who themselves sense the Lord's leadership to serve in this vital ministry.

If the bylaws designate certain persons to serve on the committee by virtue of their position, consider recommending a bylaw revision. Persons may be qualified to serve in other important offices but not qualified to serve on the pastor search committee. Church-staff members effectively serve as resource persons to the committee. However, experience shows that it is not best for them to be committee members.

Election of the Committee

Churches use many different ways to elect pastor search committees. Because of space limitations, all of the possibilities will not be discussed. The following election procedure is recommended.

Electing a pastor search committee should be done on a Sunday morning at an appropriate time after the former pastor leaves. If the pastor's departure involved difficult circumstances, such as a forced termination or death, it is probably best to postpone the election of the committee for several months. That time will give the church, under the leadership of a transitional pastor, an opportunity to process issues related to forced termination or death and to think more clearly about how to approach the future. The church will then be able to make solid practical decisions about a pastor search committee.

Prior to the Sunday designated for the election, publish the qualifications for committee members. If qualifications have not been adopted, a suitable group in the church should recommend that the church consider the suggestions presented earlier or an amended version of them for adoption. The nominating committee, the committee on committees, or the church-leadership team (church council) could function as the recommending body. This group may also recommend the total election procedure for the church's approval.

On the Sunday set aside for that purpose, the congregation nominates persons who fit the qualifications that have been previously adopted. Each member of the congregation can nominate as many persons as the church requires for the committee. For example, if you have decided that five members should compose the committee, then each church member can nominate up to five persons.

Next, the nominating committee or the committee on committees ranks nominees in order of the number of nominations received. The final tally should include persons in each of the previously approved categories, such as age group or gender.

The nominating committee or the committee on committees then takes the five to seven individuals with the most nominations and schedules a visit with each of them. They should not try to accomplish this on the telephone or by a visit in the hallway. If possible, the committee chairman and one other member should make these visits to ensure that each nominee hears the same thing. The purpose of the visit is to make sure each nominee understands what the church expects of pastor search committee members and commits to serve faithfully. If one of the initial nominees declines, contact the person with the next highest number of nominations in that qualification category.

After the committee has commitments from the correct number of pastor search committee members, give the church an opportunity to affirm the choices. Present them as a group on a Sunday morning and ask the church to affirm them as a group. Ask the newly elected committee to come to the front of the worship center immediately after the affirmation so that everyone can see them as a group. Pray for them. Print their names in the next church newsletter or Sunday bulletin with a request that all church members commit to pray for the committee daily.

Selecting Committee Officers

Chairman

In addition to possessing the qualifications listed on pages 12–13 for all committee members, the person who chairs the committee needs skill in planning and carrying out plans, a good understanding of Baptist polity, a firm grasp of the history of the church, and the respect of the congregation. The chairman serves as the facilitator of the group, not a dictator. His leadership must diligently seek to help the committee reach a decision without pushing a personal agenda. The chairman also needs to communicate with the congregation about the committee's work. The role of facilitator calls for good communication skills.

Vice-Chairman

This person needs to possess some of the same characteristics as the chairman of the committee because he must function as facilitator when the chairman is absent and must perform other duties as needed. The vice-chairman may serve as the prayer coordinator unless the committee chooses to assign that task to another person.

Secretary

The secretary does more than keep a record of the committee's actions. An additional responsibility may include executing the paperwork necessary for the committee to work effectively, such as official committee correspondence.

Prayer Coordinator

The prayer coordinator must be fervent in prayer and must be gracious in leading others to pray with fervency. The prayer coordinator works with the transitional pastor and the church staff to plan prayer times for the entire church and with the committee as it does its work. As already noted, this role may be assigned to the vice-chairman of the committee.

Understanding Theological Concepts That Guide the Committee

As the committee prepares to do its work, ask each member to read this section carefully. The committee can then discuss the biblical teachings on these topics.

The Nature of a New Testament Church

Article VI of *The Baptist Faith and Message*, adopted by the Southern Baptist Convention June 14, 2000, addresses the nature of the New Testament church. The first sentence says, "A New Testament church of the Lord Jesus Christ is an autonomous local congregation of baptized believers, associated by covenant in the faith and fellowship of the gospel; observing the two ordinances of Christ, governed by His laws, exercising the gifts, rights, and privileges invested in them by His Word, and seeking to extend the gospel to the ends of the earth."[2]

As a committee, discuss the implications of the following phrases from this definition.

1. "Autonomous local congregation of baptized believers"
2. "Associated by covenant in the faith and fellowship of the gospel"
3. "Extend the gospel to the ends of the earth"

Two passages illustrate the body of Christ, which includes all the redeemed of all ages. In Matthew 16:18 Jesus declared, "I will build My church." In Ephesians 5:25 Paul instructed husbands in Ephesus to "love your wives, just as also Christ loved the church." As a committee, read the cited passages and discuss the following questions.

1. What is the significance of the phrase "I will build My church"?
2. Who is Lord of the church?
3. Who is to "run" the church?
4. Identify evidence of Christ's love for the church.

The Bible most often uses the word *church* to refer to an assembly of Christians meeting in a specific location to carry out the Great Commission given them by Jesus, their Lord. "All authority has been given to Me in heaven and on earth. Go, therefore, and make disciples of all nations, baptizing them in the name of the Father and of the Son and of the Holy Spirit, teaching them to observe everything I have commanded you. And remember, I am with you always, to the end of the age" (Matt. 28:18-20). This mandate was addressed to the church in Jerusalem, the church in Antioch, the seven churches in Revelation, and every church in every place and every age.

"The church is God's agent of redemption in the world. It is the organism, the instrument God chose to carry His message to the world and to bring people to a saving knowledge of Christ."[3] A church that does not share the gospel as Jesus commanded is like "a restaurant that has food prepared but refuses to serve the hungry."[4] When the Great Commission is a church's driving force, five essential functions characterize the life of that church: evangelism, discipleship, fellowship, ministry, and worship. These functions focus on making disciples, maturing believers, and multiplying ministries. Steadfast commitment to these functions will result in numerical growth, spiritual transformation, ministry expansion, and kingdom advance.

As a committee, discuss the following questions.

1. If all authority in heaven and on earth was given to Jesus, who else has a right to be the authority on matters of faith and practice in the church?
2. If Jesus gave us our orders in the Great Commission, who in the church has the authority to set other priorities above evangelism, discipleship, fellowship, ministry, and worship?

God's Call to Ministry

It is very important that biblical truth about God's call to ministry, rather than church tradition, shape committee members' understanding of God's call. Therefore, committee time, individually and collectively, is well spent studying the Scriptures and learning how God has called His children to serve Him.

The Old Testament applies five different meanings to two Hebrew words for *call*. Review the passages in which these examples are found.

1. Inviting or summoning: "The LORD God called out to the man and said to him, 'Where are you?' " (Gen. 3:9).
2. Praying or calling on God: "Men began to call on the name of the LORD" (Gen. 4:26).
3. Naming something: "God called the light 'day,' and He called the darkness 'night' " (Gen. 1:5).
4. Calling into God's service: "When the LORD saw that he had gone over to look, God called out to him from the bush, 'Moses, Moses!' " (Ex. 3:4).
5. Claiming something as one's own for a particular purpose: "I have called you by your name; you are Mine" (Isa. 43:1).

In the New Testament *kaleo* is the verb form of the Greek root word for *call*. It can mean *calling or inviting someone*. Often this word refers to God's call to participate in the blessings He offers (see Rom. 8:30; 1 Cor. 1:9; 1 Thess. 2:12; Heb. 9:15).

In summary, the biblical concept of call is demonstrated as a Christian responds to God's calls to receive life through faith in the Lord of life, live daily as a ministering disciple of Christ, and accept the challenge of serving the Lord's churches in specific ways, times, and places. All Christians are called to ministry, and the kingdom of God on earth grows as they accept their callings. Pastor search committee members will accomplish committee goals more effectively if they make this period of service a time for consistently committing themselves to the callings God has for their lives. Then they can find the person God has uniquely called and equipped to be the pastor for the next period in the life of the church.

The call to ministry is always a call to prepare for ministry, both the general ministry to which all are called and the specific ministries to which individuals are called. Paul's admonition to Timothy applies to every believer: "Be diligent to present yourself approved to God, a worker who doesn't need to be ashamed, correctly teaching the word of truth" (2 Tim. 2:15). The call to preparation applies to the pastor search process in three ways.

1. New Christians are called to study God's Word, to learn from more experienced believers, and to keep their hearts open to instruction provided by the Holy Spirit.

2. As disciples are called to minister in special roles to which God directs them, they are called to gain knowledge through study and to gain wisdom through asking God and accepting what God supplies. Churches are delinquent in their care of members when they ask members to take major responsibilities in the church but do not provide training opportunities that equip them for fruitful and rewarding service.

3. Persons called to serve as pastors are called to specialized training commensurate with the call to which they have committed their lives. A call to pastoral ministry is a call to pastoral training. A person who declares that he is called to serve as a pastor but does not believe he is called to pastoral training has an inadequate concept of the call.

Michael D. Miller states, "God's call to kingdom leadership is real. To comprehend that such a call actually happens is almost impossible. Yet it does, and it happens often. This call is even more astounding when we consider who does the calling—God himself."[5] Miller describes God's call as personal, a great mystery, and life-changing. God's call is an invitation to enter the kingdom of God, as well as to live a life of holiness. God's call is to service, suffering, and abundant joy.

Take time in a committee meeting to reflect on and share with other committee members your personal experience of your call. As a committee, carefully draft some questions about God's personal calling that you will ask those you are considering as the next pastor of your church.

Biblical Profile of a Pastor

The Bible uses several different words to describe a pastor's role. The word *pastor* means *shepherd* (see Acts 20:28; Eph. 4:11; 1 Pet. 5:2). The word *bishop* means *overseer* (see Acts 20:28; Phil. 1:1; 1 Tim. 3:1; Titus 1:7; 1 Pet. 5:2). A third term, *elder*, is interchangeably used with the *pastor/shepherd* and *overseer* roles in Acts 20:17,28 and 1 Peter 5:1-3. All of these terms speak of the pastor's clear leadership role in the church.

Carefully examine the biblical standards for a pastor. Many passages of Scripture can be applied to the pastor. Some, like 1 Peter 5:3, directly apply to the way a pastor should exercise leadership. First Timothy 3:2-7 is the key passage to understand what the Bible says about a pastor's profile. Paul identified 14 characteristics of a healthy pastor.

1. Behavior that consistently shows obedience to God ("above reproach," v. 2)
2. Faithfulness in marriage ("husband of one wife," v. 2)
3. Self-control in spirit and actions ("self-controlled," v. 2)
4. Able to make appropriate decisions for the good of the kingdom of God ("sensible," v. 2)
5. Christian dignity in behavior patterns ("respectable," v. 2)
6. Genuine care for persons ("hospitable," v. 2)
7. Effective teacher of the truths of God's Word ("an able teacher," v. 2)
8. Unwillingness to let alcohol control him ("not addicted to wine," v. 3)
9. A gentle spirit ("not a bully but gentle," v. 3)
10. A peacemaker ("not quarrelsome," v. 3)
11. Actions not motivated by the love of money ("not greedy," v. 3)
12. Spiritual leader of his family ("manages his own household competently, having his children under control with all dignity," v. 4)
13. Mature in Christian belief and practice ("must not be a new convert," v. 6)
14. Credibility that attracts those outside the church ("must have a good reputation among outsiders," v .7)

Discuss the implications for your committee's work—
1. the words used to describe the role of a pastor;
2. the biblical characteristics of a healthy pastor's profile.

To the pastor profile presented in 1 Timothy 3:2-7, add Paul's list of the fruit of the Spirit found in Galatians 5:22-23: "love, joy, peace, patience, kindness, goodness, faith, gentleness, self-control." Also, in evaluating prospective pastors, carefully look for a man who is an industrious worker and who has spiritual discernment, vision, zeal for missions and evangelism, and denominational loyalty. A pastor search committee acts wisely when it includes these qualities in the profile of a prospective pastor. Your church will be blessed when these qualities are manifested day by day by the person to whom it looks for spiritual and administrative leadership.

The Priesthood of All Christians

The term *priesthood of all Christians* or *priesthood of believers* is not in the Bible, but the concept is clearly presented. Peter, writing to persecuted and scattered believers, called them "a chosen race, a royal priesthood, a holy nation, a people for His possession, so that you may proclaim the praises of the One who called you out of darkness into His marvelous light" (1 Pet. 2:9). In Revelation John addressed the seven churches in the province of Asia, writing that Christ had "made us a kingdom, priests to His God and Father—to Him be the glory and dominion forever and ever" (Rev. 1:6).

According to the writer of Hebrews, Jesus did not exalt Himself to the position of High Priest but was declared by His Father to be "a priest forever in the order of Melchizedek" (Heb. 5:6). Being a priest and sharing in the priesthood of all Christians are never the result of self-selection. Christians are priests because God has chosen them, saved them, called them, and anointed them. More than an honor bestowed, priesthood is a task assigned and a responsibility accepted. Priests are charged by the Father and empowered by His Spirit to observe and obey all of the teachings of His Son. That includes faithfully serving the Father, as Jesus did by ministering in the world in every way God directs us.

Baptists sometimes misinterpret the doctrine that all believers are priests to mean that because we are believer-priests and have direct access to Jesus Christ, we don't need anyone else to teach us or direct us. That gets translated as "I am my own authority, and I don't want anyone else having authority over me." It is true that Jesus Christ is the High Priest, the only intermediary between priests and our Heavenly Father. But it is also true that God has ordained leaders in government, leaders in churches, and leaders in families so that we may live our lives in orderly ways that honor and build up one another.

How does this principle affect the work of a pastor search committee? It means that each member has a responsibility for earnestly seeking to express the Spirit of Christ through every word spoken, every personal interaction, and every decision made. It means that each will recognize the others as priests in the kingdom of God and will show appropriate respect and deference.

As individual Christians are responsible for their beliefs and·actions, each Southern Baptist church is responsible to God, not to other churches and organizations of churches, for its actions. Each church chooses a pastor; no other entity is responsible for that choice. Each church seeks the Holy Spirit's leadership in developing a vision for the church, setting its goals, and implementing its strategies; no other entity controls such decisions.

Developing a Bond Within the Committee

Begin your work as a pastor search committee by taking some actions that will enable your committee to be more than just a group of individuals meeting together. These actions will forge a strong bond in your group so that you will care for, understand, and respect one another. They will prepare you for times when you may disagree and will help keep friction to a minimum. They will prepare you to encourage one another when the process leads to weariness and a tendency to hurry the search.

Start the bonding process in the first meeting and at the retreat described below. Let all members share something about themselves and their desires for your church. Follow this time of sharing with a time of prayer for one another, for the work of the committee, and for the church's transition time.

Committee Retreat

To further the process of bonding, plan a pastor search committee retreat away from the church, if possible. The retreat may be a full day, two half days, or several two- or three-hour meetings. A retreat offers the opportunity to develop and deepen a bond of fellowship among committee members. Use the retreat to learn how a pastor search committee functions effectively and to decide on committee covenants.

Provide refreshments and lunch on site to maximize the use of this important time. Tool 1, "Pastor Search Committee Retreat," offers a suggested full-day agenda. The agenda can be adapted for a different schedule. Arrange well in advance to have a copy of *Pastor Search Committee Handbook* for each committee member.

Prior planning will ensure the success of the retreat. Use this handbook as a training guide. If you need additional assistance, invite an outside person to orient your committee to its work. Your associational director of missions, state convention's church-minister relations director, or a transitional pastor can help you. He can either lead the orientation himself or suggest someone who can. Information for contacting Baptist state conventions is provided in tool 2.

Committee Covenant

Decide on covenant agreements that committee members will honor. To get the process started, consider the following covenant possibilities. Add to this list or change the wording, but include these important understandings in your covenant.

1. *A covenant of ethical behavior.* Agree that each committee member will treat one another in a manner consistent with the ethical standards that characterized Jesus' life.
2. *A covenant of spiritual preparation.* Agree to make Bible study and prayer ongoing personal priorities.
3. *A covenant of prayer.* Pledge to pray for one another and for the church.
4. *A covenant of unity.* Agree to work in unity, not regarding self as having more value than others, "diligently keeping the unity of the Spirit with the peace that binds us" (Eph. 4:3).
5. *A covenant of honesty and openness.* Agree to be honest and open with one another, always seeking the Holy Spirit's guidance so that the fruit of the Spirit (see Gal. 5:22-23) will characterize the committee members.
6. *A covenant of confidentiality.* Agree that what is discussed within the committee will stay within the committee so that there can be complete honesty and openness among members. Agree on what specific information will be released to other church members and family members.
7. *A covenant of faithfulness.* Agree that you will remain faithful to the church and its ministries while your committee does its work. As a result, church members will continue to have confidence in the committee, and you can more effectively interpret the church to prospective pastors.

Tool 3 is a sample "Pastor Search Committee Covenant of Agreements." Reproduce copies for members to sign. Keep the signed copies in the committee's official records.

Developing and Adopting Committee Guidelines

During the retreat or in a second committee meeting, review the actions that follow. Adopt as many of the guidelines as you can during the retreat and plan to complete the process in a subsequent meeting. Make sure the guidelines become part of your committee's permanent documents.

Study the Church's Constitution and Bylaws

"Selecting the Pastor Search Committee," pages 11–14, stated the importance of following the procedures stipulated in the church's bylaws. Bylaws may also contain operating guidelines for a pastor search committee to follow. If you find specific items there, follow them or ask the church's permission to deviate from them. If you don't find any guidelines in the bylaws or in other official church documents, develop your own.

Adopt a Search Process

Read the suggested search process in phases 2, 3, and 4 of this handbook. After considering the different aspects of this process, determine whether to follow this model in its entirety, modify it, or use another one. After you decide, explain the process to the congregation. Church members can then ask questions for clarification. This step will save some questions later in the process.

Clarify the Role of the Church Staff

The relationship of the church staff—full-time, part-time, or volunteer—to the pastor-search process is very important. Although staff members should not be members of the search committee, they can help the committee gather information about the church. They can keep the committee up-to-date on what is happening in the church. Survey staff members about what they want their pastor to be. At the appropriate point in your search process, have the staff meet with the candidate. Beyond this the staff should not take an active role in the search process so that they will not be distracted from their primary responsibilities. The staff can best help by focusing on their ministry roles, thereby providing continuity and stability to the fullest extent possible during the search process.

The church needs to determine in advance the pastor's role in relationship to employed staff. The committee will need to be honest and thorough with a prospective pastor in evaluating the staff's effectiveness. If any staff members have been contentious or divisive in the staff and/or the church, the personnel committee should take action to solve the problem *before* a new pastor is called. Forcing a new pastor to deal with old, unresolved problems early in his ministry is unjust. The church needs to have a policy that is clear to existing staff and the prospective pastor as to whether staff can continue their service to the church or whether the new pastor can replace them.

Develop Communication Guidelines

One of the most critical tasks in the search process is keeping the church informed and receiving information from the church. Decide who will function as the official spokesperson for the committee. Although the chairman usually assumes this role, this does not prevent other committee members from giving reports to the entire church or to segments of the church. However, the congregation should look to the chairman for official words from the committee.

Plan to make regular reports to the church. You may do this during a Sunday-morning worship time as well as at the church's regular business sessions. At least once a month the committee should report to the church.

If your church has a newsletter, the committee can keep the church informed in a monthly progress report. For example, you may report that the committee is gathering or considering prospect profiles. Because you have already shared with the church the entire process your committee has adopted, the congregation can follow your progress as you share with it.

Prepare a Committee Budget

Get the church's approval to spend money on appropriate committee expenses. In arranging for funds for the committee's travel to meet with a candidate and/ or to bring him and his wife to visit the community, the committee chairman should inform the person issuing checks of the critical nature of confidentiality. Consider the following expenses.

1. Committee materials—the cost of duplicating needed forms, surveys, mailings to the congregation, and letters about candidates
2. Telephone calls—calls made seeking names of prospective pastors as well as calls about candidates
3. Postal box—the rental of a post-office box to provide greater confidentiality than using the church address
4. Travel expenses—expenses needed to cover travel involved in considering a candidate, including car or plane expense, hotel costs, and meal costs
5. Candidate expenses and travel—the cost of bringing a prospective pastor and his family to your church field when that time comes. Because you may have to do this with more than one person, the congregation should understand the expenses involved.

Develop a Proposed Pastor-Church Covenant of Relationship

Churches often use secular terms like *job description* and *contract* in forging a new pastor-church relationship, but the relationship is best referred to as a *covenant*. Churches enter legally binding contracts with secular organizations or individuals outside the church and are liable to courts of law. Churches enter covenants within the church, agreements that should never have to be enforced by secular laws.

A pastor-church covenant of relationship should include these elements:
1. What the pastor commits to the relationship
2. What the church commits to the relationship
3. The pastor's work schedule
4. Salary, housing, benefits, and expenses
5. Vacation and sabbatical

Tool 4 is a sample "Pastor-Church Covenant of Relationship." Use it as a starter in preparing a covenant that honestly expresses the commitments of both church and prospective pastor. Tool 5 further clarifies the pastor's salary, housing, benefits, and expenses. Tool 6 is a a checklist to assist the pastor search committee in spelling out what the church will provide for the pastor. Work with the personnel, budget, and other appropriate committees to answer the questions. These three tools deal with issues that can lay the foundation for a positive, effective, and lasting relationship between the pastor and the congregation. Taking time to clarify these specifics is crucial.

Obtain Authority from the Church

Before continuing the work of your committee, request and receive approval from the church for the committee budget and for the pastor-church covenant of relationship. If necessary, include a recommendation for the pastor's authority and relationship with the church staff. Because these constitute critical areas in the life of the church, give adequate time to prayerfully and carefully consider what you will recommend.

1. Adapted from Henry A. Virkler, *Choosing a New Pastor: The Complete Handbook* (Nashville: Oliver Nelson, 1992), 210–15. Used by permission.
2. *The Baptist Faith and Message: A Statement Adopted by the Southern Baptist Convention,* June 14, 2000 (Nashville: LifeWay Christian Resources, 2000), 13.
3. Gene Mims, *Kingdom Principles for Church Growth,* revised and expanded (Nashville: LifeWay Press, 2001), 17. Out of print.
4. Ibid., 22.
5. Michael D. Miller, *Kingdom Leadership: A Call to Christ-Centered Leadership* (Nashville: Convention Press, 1996), 25. Out of print.

Phase 2

How Do We Gather the Information We Need?

Developing Profiles

Before requesting profiles from associational, state, and national sources of information, prepare a profile that represents the perceptions of the church and the committee about the kind of pastor the church needs. Also prepare profiles of the church and the community. These profiles will help those from whom you request information nominate candidates who are most likely to be seriously considered by the committee. They will also help the committee more quickly process the pastor profiles received and identify candidates most likely to be a good pastor-church match.

Profile of a Prospective Pastor

First, find out what the church desires in a pastor. Invite the congregation to respond in writing. Use the model provided in tool 7, "Pastor Search Congregational Survey," or develop a profile of your own. You may get the best results by letting members of the committee explain this survey to the Adult and Youth Sunday School departments. Allow a week for the congregation to complete the survey. A separate tally of committee members' surveys can reveal any significant differences fom the total congregation's.

A congregational assembly in which church members have the opportunity to voice their opinions may enhance the written profile. The person leading this assembly should do so as an impartial moderator. If you have a transitional pastor, he may preside and guide a process that allows each member and age group to hear what others in the church think and feel. Comments should be limited to what members desire for the future of their church without references to former pastors. Remember that the purpose of this experience is to hear personal perceptions, not to evaluate their merits. Listen nonjudgmentally.

If you have a congregational meeting for this purpose, consider the following practical matters.

1. Provide child care.
2. Conduct the meeting away from the worship center.
3. If microphones are needed, provide floor microphones or a roving microphone so that people will not have to come to the front.
4. Set a time limit, such as one hour, for the meeting.

5. Conduct the meeting graciously and prayerfully.

6. If possible, have a time of fellowship and refreshments after the meeting.

Use the survey and information from the meeting to compile a profile of a prospective pastor. Use this profile when asking for profiles of and information about prospective pastors to consider.

Sometimes understanding a person's attitudes and behaviors related to job responsibilities is difficult. Tool 8, "Position Insights Profile," is an excellent instrument to help a search committee discern the ideal behavioral qualities for a position and compare them to the same set of qualities demonstrated by candidates for that role. You can use this tool in conjunction with other evaluation and search activities to help simplify the very subjective nature of assessing a person's God-given communication styles, personal strengths, and attitudinal preferences.

The search committee should use "Position Insights Profile" to identify the behavioral demands of the position itself, not the behavior of the pastor. Later, each top candidate for the position will be asked to complete "Leading from Your Strengths Profile," which reveals his ways of dealing with people and tasks. The committee can then compare both sets of information to provide another perspective (in addition to life and work experiences, education, and so forth) on a candidate's potential fit with the specific position. Instructions about obtaining and using these resources are provided in tool 8.

Profile of the Church

If you have chosen a transitional pastor, he can lead the church through most of the first four steps of preparation for calling a new pastor (see list at top of p. 11) before the pastor search committee begins the search process. A person who receives training as a transitional pastor learns how to help a church assess its strengths and weaknesses, develop its ministries according to Great Commission priorities, and allocate its resources according to ministry priorities instead of traditions or customs. That process helps clarify the church profile in terms of its understanding of mission and appropriate strategies.

You can use the sample profile in tool 9 to develop a demographic profile of church membership. Use a method of distribution that will generate the most data for producing an accurate composite (profile) of church membership.

Obtain a copy of each of the past five Annual Church Profiles of your church. These may be available in the church files, since the church clerk or a staff member compiled the information and provided it to the office of the associational director of missions. If they are not in the church files, obtain these from your association, state convention, or LifeWay Christian Resources. The composite profile developed from tool 9, "Demographic Profile of Church

Membership," and the information in the Annual Church Profile provide a good picture of the church for the committee and for prospective pastors.

Profile of the Community

Finding a pastor who matches the needs of your church and community serves as a priority for your committee. To accomplish this, you will want to develop a community profile. If your church has a transitional pastor, he can guide you in this process. A good community profile includes the following information.

1. Population and ethnic makeup (from census data)
2. Type of community (suburban, rural, inner city)
3. Socioeconomic status of the community (from census data on family income)
4. Special situations of the community (tourism, major industries)
5. Schools
6. Health-care facilities
7. Community transition (growing, stable, declining)
8. Urban center to which the community relates
9. Other churches ministering effectively in the community
10. Major community social services

Assign the development of a profile of the community to the committee member who knows the most about community-information resources. The committee should review and revise the profile as needed to represent the understandings of the full committee.

Gathering Prospect Profiles

Some profiles (résumés) will arrive at the church when the word of your pastor's leaving becomes known. These usually come from or on behalf of persons who are not presently serving a church or pastors who desire, for whatever reasons, to relocate. In processing them, be careful to ascertain why the applicants have taken this initiative.

Acknowledge each profile as it is received with a letter of thanks and a request for prayer for the committee and church. This particularly holds true for profiles that come from individuals outside your church.

Sources for Profiles of Prospective Pastors

1. *Director of missions.* Contact your associational director of missions. Inform him that you are seeking a pastor and wish to receive copies of profiles he believes may be a good match for your church. Provide him with copies of the profile of a prospective pastor, the profile of the church, and the profile of the community that your committee has developed. You may also contact the directors of missions in associations immediately adjacent to yours.

2. *State-convention offices.* Each state convention has a person who assists pastor search committees. In some states this person may have additional responsibilities. Contact your state-convention offices (see tool 2) and ask to be put in touch with the person who works with pastor search committees (sometimes called a church-minister-relations director). Be prepared to provide copies of the profile of a prospective pastor, the profile of the church, and the profile of the community.

3. *Baptist seminaries.* Southern Baptist seminaries (see tool 10) form another rich source for names of prospective pastors. Provide the three profiles to one or more seminary placement directors and invite them to provide you with pastor profiles that match the profiles you sent them.

4. *Other pastors, congregational members, and miscellaneous sources.* Church members may want to submit the names of prospective pastors. Ask them to provide as much information as possible about the person, including a profile, if possible. Pastors in the local area and other people may also send names. If they do not have profiles of those they suggest, ask them to provide the information you need to contact the candidates.

Biographical-Profile Format

A sample "Biographical Profile," provided in tool 11, may be adapted by the pastor search committee as desired. Developing a standard biographical profile (résumé) format will ensure that you have the same basic information on all you will consider.

Some prospects need guidance in preparing a profile. Ask for information that is missing.

Cutoff Date for Receiving Profiles

Set a six- to eight-week cutoff date for receiving profiles. This deadline will establish a date when the committee will begin looking at the first group of profiles. It does not mean you will no longer accept profiles but that you will start the process of review and will hold the others until you have finished considering the group whose profiles were received by the cutoff date.

Phase 3

How Do We Let God Lead Us to the Right Pastor?

Although each phase of the pastor-selection process is very important, no phase should be immersed in prayer more than phase 3. Human knowledge and judgment are inadequate. Only spiritual discernment is sufficient, and spiritual discernment is given to those who earnestly seek it: "Call to Me and I will answer you and tell you great and wondrous things you do not know" (Jer. 33:3). This is a time to talk to God and listen to Him.

Study and Evaluate Profiles

Give all committee members copies of each pastor profile received by the committee before the meeting in which they will be evaluated so that members can review them in advance. Tool 12 provides a form to use in evaluating the prospective pastors.

Consider Priority Areas on the Profiles

Look for matches of the biblical, church, and community profiles with the pastors' biographical profiles. If there is any serious disconnect with a particular candidate, God may be guiding you to consider that prospect no longer. Following are the primary areas to consider.

1. *Philosophy of ministry.* Consider how he sees his role in the church and his priorities for the way the church carries out its ministry.
2. *Experience.* Consider the years of service and the types of experiences in ministry, such as the size and community setting of the churches he has served. Carefully look for ways that affirm he could be a match. Generally, the longer a person's experience has focused on one particular setting, the more his way of doing ministry is influenced by that setting.
3. *Tenure.* Consider the average tenure in each of his church positions. If a pastor has stayed only a short time in previous pastorates (other than student pastorates), include this pattern as an important topic of conversation if the committee interviews him.
4. *Education.* Compare each candidate's educational qualifications to the information about educational preference provided on the congregation's pastor profile. As you consider this area, consult tool 13 for information on academic degrees. To verify educational credentials, call or write the registrar of each college, university, and/or seminary. Also examine the area

on the profile that gives the candidate's involvement in continuing education, such as seminars, workshops, college, and/or seminary-extension programs. This information will reveal the prospective pastor's desire to continue growing in knowledge and skills.

5. *Family background.* Consider the prospective pastor's family background and his present family situation. Is he married? Will your church consider a pastor who has never been married or who is widowed? Will you consider a pastor who has been divorced? If he is married, do he and his wife have children at home? How many children do they have, and does the number make a difference? Does the church have specific expectations in these areas of family life?

6. *Other interests.* Considering the prospective pastor's hobbies will reveal whether he lives a balanced lifestyle. Many pastors experience great difficulty fulfilling their many responsibilities and expectations while still having meaningful free time. The most effective pastors understand the part holistic wellness plays in life and work, and they make time for work, play, exercise, and hobbies.

Rank the Profiles

The importance of prayer cannot be overemphasized as the committee begins to prefer distinguish prospects from others and, finally, one candidate above all others. Ask all church members to pray that God will grant spiritual discernment during this time.

Don't overlook possible candidates who are not willing to send a profile because they are content where they are serving. Some pastors are not willing to send a profile until you focus only on them.

The next step in the search process is to rank the profiles. After considering them prayerfully and carefully, rank them according to the individuals' conformity to what your church needs. Identify 7 to 10 who seem best qualified. One way to do this is to ask each committee member to rank the 10 strongest profiles before the next meeting, ranking the strongest 1 and continuing through 10. In that meeting committee members will compare rankings and will discuss them until they reach a consensus on the 7 to 10 most impressive profiles for your church at this time in its history.

Choose Three to Five Prospects for Further Consideration

The next step is choosing the top three to five prospects from the list of prioritized profiles. At this point you should decide solely on the basis of candidates' profiles. Create a separate file for each of them. Place "Confidential Personnel Information" notice, provided in tool 14, on the front cover or as the first page of each file.

In selecting the five, follow the same procedure you used in the first ranking of profiles. Prayerfully seek God's leadership both collectively and individually as you make these critical decisions.

Write to the Top Prospects and Request Additional Information

Because your correspondence will probably be on your church's letterhead, use only the prospect's home address for correspondence.

1. Inform each prospect of the committee's desire to consider him further.
2. Ask for any information you do not already have that your committee considers necessary.
3. Request audios and/or videos of two sermons he has preached in the past two years.
4. If a candidate did not include references with the profile, request the desired number of references you may contact for information.
5. Send the candidate a copy of "Reference Release," found in tool 15, with a self-addressed, stamped envelope.
6. Send information about your church and community. Suggestions about what to include are provided in tool 16, "Portfolio of Church and Community." You may decide to send some of this information only when you have narrowed your focus to one prospect.
7. If in phase 2 the committee used "Position Insights Profile" (tool 8) to construct a profile of the pastor you seek, ask each of the five prospects to complete "Leading from Your Strengths Profile." Use the instructions in tool 8.

Write to the Persons You Will Not Consider at This Stage

After writing to the top candidates, also write letters to all others from whom you have received profiles (if they know they were being considered). Inform them that your committee will not consider them at this time. Thank them for allowing your church to consider the information they provided. Tell them you as a committee have prayed for them, asking God to guide and bless them in ministry. Ask them to pray for your church at this critical time in its life. Keep all information in a secure file in case God leads you to reconsider one of these candidates.

Focus on One Prospect

You have now reached the point of selecting one person on whom to focus attention. Most search committees testify that churches should consider only one prospect at a time. To consider more than one at a time can lead to division among committee members and can delay the decision-making process.

The prayer coordinator should schedule a special time of prayer, perhaps devoting a complete meeting to this purpose, before the committee decides on the prospect to consider first. Prayer can help the committee come to a consensus in a way that is free of coercion.

Select One Candidate

Carefully review all of the information for each of the top candidates:

1. "Biographical Profile" (see tool 11)
2. Audios and/or videos (see tool 21)
3. "Leading from Your Strengths Profile" (see tool 8)

Compare this information to your church, community, pastor, and Position Insights profiles. Ask each committee member to rank the top three candidates. Compare rankings and reach a consensus on the top candidate.

Remember that you are still in the consideration phase. Deciding to consider one man at this time does not necessarily mean that you will choose him as your pastor.

Check References

Now that you will focus your attention on one prospect, begin the process of gathering reference information. To obtain written references, use a letter similar to "Letter for Written References" (tool 17). Enclose "Character-Reference Inquiry" (tool 18) and "Reference Release" (tool 15), signed and returned to you by the prospect you are considering.

"Character-Reference Inquiry" asks respondents to provide the names of other persons you may choose to contact as references. As soon as you receive these additional names, arrange a telephone interview with each person. These references may provide new data or confirm the information you received through mail responses to "Character-Reference Inquiry."

"Letter for Telephone Interviews" (tool 19) can be used to notify the references you will call to interview. Enclose a copy of "Reference Release" (tool 15) to ensure the person being interviewed that you are acting with the approval of the prospective pastor. Use "Character-Reference Inquiry" (tool 18) to guide the telephone interview. Be attentive to the respondent's tone of voice and any hesitation in answering questions. Listen for what is said as well as what is not said. Take thorough notes.

Too often pastor search committee members have said in hindsight, "If only we had taken the references provided us more seriously instead of being overly persuaded by the prospect's personality, we could have avoided the problems our church has encountered." Carefully analyze the reference data, looking for patterns in responses that might raise red flags of caution. Don't ignore one person's negative comments about a prospect. That person might be the only one who is willing to be forthright with the committee. Ask each reference for additional names of those who know the prospective pastor. These secondary references are often the most valuable to the committee.

Interview the Prospect and His Wife

After you have chosen a person to consider first, have carefully considered all the reference information available, and have found no information that cautions you about proceeding, arrange an interview with the prospect and his wife. Ideally, this interview would occur in the area of the church where he presently serves. However, if he lives far from your area, it may be more cost effective for the two of them to travel the greater distance. That would mean a meeting place near your community, where it is not likely you will be seen by members of your church or his children. Choose a time when you would not feel rushed during the interview. Tool 20 provides suggested questions for the interview. This interview can also be conducted as a conference phone call with the candidate and the full committee.

Decide Whether to Continue with This Prospect

Based on the comparison of profiles, the references, and the first interview, the committee must decide whether to continue considering this prospect. Again, much prayer for God's guidance is imperative.

If you decide that he will no longer be a candidate, immediately inform him with a telephone call, followed by a letter. In all communication with him, thank him for the privilege of considering him, assure him of your continuing prayer for his ministry, and ask for his prayerful support of your church in this strategic time of decision making.

If you will continue to consider him, proceed with the following steps.

Hear the Prospect Preach

Contact the prospect to learn whether he wants to continue the process. If so, plan for the full committee to hear the prospect preach in his church, if possible. Find out if he will be preaching in his church on a Sunday morning when as many members of your committee as possible can *discreetly* attend a worship service. Assure him that you will be careful not to cause any more interruption in his ministry than is necessary. If he does not believe your visit would be in the best interest of his church at this time, ask whether he would preach in another church in the area at a time your committee can attend.

A word of caution: some committees start hearing several prospects preach early in the process. This can lead the committee to focus primarily on preaching, while neglecting other important abilities of a prospective pastor. This approach can also waste valuable travel time and money.

Under some circumstances, when the prospect lives a great distance from the church, it may be necessary to depend on video presentations of the prospect's preaching. Only with videos are you able to observe pulpit manner-isms that may support the message or distract from it.

Tool 21, "Sermon Evaluation," provides help for preparing a written evaluation of the prospect after committee members have heard him preach. Under no circumstances should they fill out the evaluation during the service. To do so would be indiscreet and impolite. Plan for the committee to meet and process their evaluations as soon as possible after hearing the sermon.

Interview the Prospect and His Wife Again

This second interview takes place in the committee's church community but not in the church. The purposes are to let the couple get to know the church area and to develop rapport between them and the committee. A good place to have this meeting is in a committee member's home. It should not be scheduled on Sunday.

Show the couple the community in which the church is located. Include significant places in your town or city. If you have a parsonage, show it to them. If you don't have a parsonage, show the couple some residential communities in the area.

Allow ample time for questions and dialogue. Share the committee's schedule for further consideration. Agree on a time when the prospect can tell the committee whether he is willing to pursue the consideration.

This is the time to introduce documents that facilitate background checks on the prospect. Although you may feel reluctant to deal with credit and criminal issues, background checks are important. Unfortunately, such investigations have become a necessity in our society. Before using the documents suggested in the toolbox to conduct background checks, you may wish to have an attorney review them in light of your state's laws to ensure that their use poses no potential legal problems. Handle these matters with diplomacy and dignity. By this time the committee and prospect should have developed a relationship of confidentiality and trust.

Give the prospect a copy of the following.
1. Tool 22, "Credit and Legal Information Release"
2. Tool 23, "Request for Criminal-Records Check and Authorization"
3. Tool 24, "Letter to Prospective Pastor About Questionnaire"
4. Tool 25, "Prospective-Pastor Questionnaire"

Inform the pastor that the committee will use this information to protect the church only in the unlikely event that litigation should result from the pastor's employment. Let him know that after your committee has reviewed the material, it will be kept in confidential files for review only by church officers. Obtaining this information does not imply distrust; the action is designed to heighten trust.

Conduct a Negotiation Conference with the Prospect

Prior to this meeting, the pastor search committee should complete the background checks and should work with the committee or committees that propose budget recommendations to the church. General agreements should be made about salary, housing, benefits, and expenses the pastor search committee may discuss with the prospective pastor (tools 5–6). In addition, the pastor search committee should review and revise, if desired, tool 4, "Pastor-Church Covenant of Relationship," to express its understanding of what the pastor and the church can bring to a healthy, long-term church ministry. Mail the prospect a copy of "Pastor-Church Covenant of Relationship" that the church has approved. Request that he study it and be prepared to suggest other considerations.

If after prayerful consideration both the prospect and your committee decide it is the Lord's will to continue, invite him to come to the church community again or to meet in a neutral location as you did for the second interview. Explain that the primary purpose of this visit is to work on a pastor-church covenant of relationship.

Discuss together what the pastor can bring to the relationship. Invite suggestions for revision. Do the same thing with what the church agrees to bring to the relationship. Does he see the document as comprehensive of the support the church should provide the pastor, or should there be additions or deletions? Negotiate recommendations that are negotiable. As much as you can, finalize an agreement on these matters.

This meeting will also provide an opportunity to clarify any matters that may have surfaced in the background checks.

Next, discuss the section on work schedule. Work with the document until both parties are comfortable with it. Follow that with discussions about the pastor's salary and benefits. Be careful not to give the impression that the committee is empowered to make financial decisions for the church at this point. The committee will get a sense of what the pastor feels he needs for his family to live in the community and to maintain a standard of living commensurate with community standards and his position in the community. Conduct the discussion so that committee members and the prospective pastor develop a clear understanding of each other's expectations and desires. Come to a clear agreement on the items the committee will recommend to the church. You will find additional help in tool 5, "Pastor's Salary, Housing, Benefits, and Expenses," and in tool 6, "Checklist for Pastor's Salary, Housing, Benefits, and Expenses."

After the meeting the committee will review the information developed and propose to the committee responsible for budget recommendations any desired changes in budget provisions for the pastor's salary and benefits. Then notify the prospect of the proposal that the budget committee will recommend to the church.

Decide Whether to Continue with the Presentation/Recommendation Process

If your analysis of the process thus far indicates that you should not continue with this prospect, graciously notify him by telephone as soon as possible. Return the confidential documents you received from him, review the information on the remaining top prospects, and start the process again. Follow the same procedure if the prospect informs the committee that he does not wish to continue the negotiation.

If after fervent, focused prayer and careful analysis of all the information gathered in the preceding processes the committee feels God's leadership to take the final and most critical step, begin preparing for the pastor and his family to visit the church. In a telephone conversation between the committee chairman and the prospective pastor, schedule a date for the visit. Inform him of the schedule of events during the visit. Tell him the plan for informing him of the church's response to the committee's recommendation. Inquire whether their children will accompany him and his wife so that you can properly plan for their visit.

Notify the appropriate church leaders of the date and events that will accompany this visit of the prospective pastor and his family. Give them adequate time to make arrangements for the church to accord the special visitors the finest hospitality possible.

Phase 4

How Should We Present the Prospective Pastor?

The Prospective Pastor and His Family Visit the Church

Members of the pastor search committee have agreed that God has led them to this prospect. He has agreed that he and his wife feel God's leading to serve the church. Now it is time for the church to decide whether it feels that he is called and equipped by God to provide pastoral leadership for the church.

The Church Learns About the Prospective Pastor

Consider these options for informing the church about the prospective pastor and the plans for his visit.

1. Provide an attractive brochure with biographical information and a picture of the pastor and his family, as well as other information. Have the pastor search committee report on the Sunday before the prospective pastor's visit. Committee members may wish to testify about their reasons for believing him to be the one God has led them to recommend. The committee may distribute an unsigned copy of the proposed "Pastor-Church Covenant of Relationship" (tool 4). Some churches include the proposed salary and benefits, but many churches do not. This option provides church members all the information they need before meeting the prospect and hearing the message God has placed in his heart for the occasion.

2. Announce the basic information about the prospective pastor's visit the week before he and his family are to visit the church. Ask the church to pray for this experience. Print an article in the weekly church newsletter or in a letter sent to church members, along with a picture of the prospective pastor and his family. Tell church members how the recommendation, vote, and announcements of results will be handled.

The Prospect and His Wife Meet with Church Groups

During the weekend of the prospective pastor's visit, provide opportunities for him and his wife to meet with strategic church groups, such as deacons, the church leadership team (church council), the staff, and youth. The committee and/or the prospective pastor may want to schedule one-to-one meetings between the prospective pastor and staff members and other church leaders. Announce this schedule in advance and encourage these church groups to make the meetings a priority.

The Committee Hosts a Churchwide Reception

On the Saturday evening of the weekend visit, provide an informal, church-wide fellowship time in which the prospective pastor, his wife, and his family can meet and visit with members and friends of the church. Make it a casual time without a formal receiving line. Committee members can guide the process so that a few individuals do not monopolize his time.

Invite the prospective pastor to briefly share his spiritual journey. Then provide a question-and-answer period so that the congregation can ask him questions. If the church has a transitional pastor, he can preside over this dialogue session so that it is gracious and informative. If there is no transitional pastor, the committee chairman may preside.

The Prospective Pastor Preaches at the Morning Worship Service

With the cooperation of the church staff, plan a worship service that allows the visitor to have maximal time to preach. As early as possible, provide him with a copy of the order of worship and indicate who will lead the prayers and introduce the guest preacher. Also inform him of the way the invitation time is normally handled when a guest preaches.

The Committee Recommends the Prospective Pastor to the Church

The Time of the Recommendation

The chairman of the pastor search committee makes the recommendation to the church. Good reasons exist for doing this at the end of the service in which the prospect preaches. Some churches may choose to do this at a later date, such as the following week. If you delay the vote, however, some who were present the day the prospect spoke may not be able to attend the day the vote is taken. Conversely, some who did not meet the prospect or hear him preach will be present and vote without some important information.

The Church Vote

Conduct the vote according to the church's established procedures. Usually, that means ballots are given only to church members. After the service in which the prospective pastor preaches, he and his family will leave the church.

The congregation is immediately informed of the results of the vote. Depending on the size of the membership voting, if the vote is by secret ballot, the congregation may not have the results before adjourning. At the next service after the vote, let the congregation know the results. Print the results in the church newsletter if you have one.

If members accept the committee's recommendation, the church is ready to move into a new era of ministry. If they don't, the committee begins the search process again with the next person on its list of top candidates. The congregation's disagreement means that not enough members interpreted the information available to them the same way committee members interpreted its information. The committee must then review its communication with the church to determine whether improvements can be made to prepare for future recommendations.

The Prospective Pastor Is Informed of Church Action

Inform the prospective pastor according to the prearranged plan. It is probably best for him to receive the information after returning home, especially if his children accompany their parents on the church visit. If not, he may wait in the community until he receives a report from the committee chairman.

Ask for a verbal decision from the candidate and a follow-up letter confirming this decision. Send him a copy of tool 4, "Pastor-Church Covenant of Relationship," with the appropriate signatures.

The Church Is Informed of the Prospective Pastor's Response

As soon as possible, verbally report to the church the candidate's decision. Call the congregation to prayer, thanking God for providing a pastor to lead in the next phase of the church's journey. Also begin to pray daily for the new pastor and his family as they leave one church and begin ministry with your church.

▶▶▶ **Phase 5**

How Do We Give the Pastor a Good Start?

A Time of Celebration

Use these and other ideas to welcome the new pastor and his family and to ease their transition to your church.

Help the Family Feel Welcome
Make the new pastor and his family's arrival a time of celebration.
1. Ask members of the church to write welcome letters.
2. Ask children to draw welcome pictures.
3. Provide meals for the pastor and his family during the move.
4. Provide child care for the family during the move.
5. Fill the pastor's pantry with food.
6. Arrange for a special prayer commitment for the pastor, his family, and the church during the first month of the transition.

Plan an Installation Service
Plan an installation service for the first Sunday-morning worship service (or a special afternoon service to accommodate guests) after the new pastor comes to your church or soon thereafter. This formal welcome to your church can impress on the congregation the new pastor's importance in the life of the church and community. It can also serve as a formal break with the tenure of the former pastor. Ideas for planning an installation service are provided in "Service of Installation and Commitment" (tool 26) and in "Installation Service" (tool 27).

Notify the Association and State Convention
Notify your local Baptist association of the church's action in calling a new pastor. Inform the associational director of missions of your new pastor's arrival date and of his first Sunday with the church. Invite him to participate in the installation service.

Notify your Baptist state convention by sending information about your new pastor and his family to the Baptist state paper and the church-minister-relations director in your state convention's office (see tool 2). Include in this information the name of each family member and the family's address, phone number(s), email address, and fax number.

The First Year of Service

The search committee should plan a meeting between the new pastor and the church's pastor-church relations committee (or the personnel committee). The meeting's purpose is for the pastor search committee to review with the pastor-church relations committee, in the new pastor's presence, "Pastor-Church Covenant of Relationship" and any other formal or informal agreement the pastor search committee may have entered with the pastor. This joint review also provides encouragement, affirmation, and mutual feedback.

These two committees can help the congregation understand what this first year of transition means for the new pastor and his family. If the church has not welcomed a new pastor for several years, many members may not realize the time required to make a good transition or the importance of their positive contribution to the process.

Pastor-Church Relations Team

If your church does not have a pastor-church relations team, this is a good time to elect one. This team fosters ongoing, positive relationships between the pastor and other groups in the church. The members encourage and affirm. They serve as an advisory group on matters of relationships and as an accountability group that always prays for the pastor. Information about a pastor-church relations team is provided in tool 28.

Orientation to the Community

The transitional pastor, a member of the pastor search committee, or a member of the pastor-church relations team should make appointments and introduce the new pastor to various community leaders. These might include the associational director of missions, the chairman of the local pastor's conference, city and county officials, principals of schools served by the church, and hospital administrators.

Women on the pastor search committee or on the pastor-church relations team could take the wife on a tour of the community, identifying various service providers. They could also host a brunch or a tea to help the pastor's wife get acquainted and become more comfortable.

First impressions are often lasting ones. Thoughtfulness, graciousness, and generosity are Christlike qualities that can be expressed by offering to help during unpacking and by providing meals during the time of adjustment.

Annual Performance Review

A yearly performance review allows the pastor and the church to assess how each is living up to "Pastor-Church Covenant of Relationship" (tool 4). A sample performance review in tool 29 is provided for your personnel committee's annual use. Adapt the sample to fit your church's covenant. Each committee member should complete a copy. The committee chairman should guide a process for coming to a committee consensus for each item. Only the consensus report is shared with the pastor.

Pastor-Appreciation Day

Plan for Pastor-Appreciation Day to become part of your church's ongoing calendar of activities. Many churches schedule this event on a Sunday in October. You can obtain information about how to conduct such an event by contacting your state convention's church-minister-relations director (see tool 2). The pastor's anniversary with the church and his birthday provide other opportunities for special expressions of appreciation. A pastor, like any church member, thrives on appreciation.

Toolbox

PASTOR SEARCH COMMITTEE RETREAT

8:00 a.m.	Fellowship time with coffee and juice
8:15	Scripture reading and prayer
8:30	Personal testimonies of members' spiritual pilgrimages and personal dreams for the church and its new pastor
9:30	Break
9:45	Overview of *Pastor Search Committee Handbook*
10:00	Discussion of "Understanding Theological Concepts That Guide the Committee" (phase 1, p. 15)
10:45	Break
11:00	Discussion of "Committee Covenant" (phase 1, pp. 20–21) and "Pastor Search Committee Covenant of Agreements" (tool 3)
11:45	Agreement on committee covenant
12:00 noon	Lunch
12:45 p.m.	Discussion of "Developing and Adopting Committee Guidelines" (phase 1, p. 21)
1:30	Discussion of phase 2 of the search process
2:00	Break
2:15	Discussion of phase 3 of the search process
2:45	Discussion of phases 4–5 of the search process
3:15	Break
3:30	Agreement on committee guidelines and recommendations to the church
4:15	Prayer for the work of the committee and the church
5:00	Adjourn

TOOL 2

DIRECTORY OF BAPTIST STATE CONVENTIONS

Alabama
Alabama Baptist Convention State Board of Missions
PO Box 681970
Prattville, AL 36068-1970
Phone: 800-264-1225
Website: www.alsbom.org

Alaska
Alaska Baptist Convention
1750 O'Malley Road
Anchorage, AK 99507
Phone: 800-883-9627
Website: www.alaskabaptistconvention.com

Arizona
Arizona Southern Baptist Convention
2240 North Hayden Road, Suite 100
Scottsdale, AZ 85257
Phone: 800-687-2431
Website: www.azsobaptist.org

Arkansas
Arkansas Baptist State Convention
10 Remington Drive
Little Rock, AR 72204
Phone: 501-376-4791
Website: www.absc.org

California
California Southern Baptist Convention
678 East Shaw Avenue
Fresno, CA 93710-7704
Phone: 559-229-9533
Website: www.csbc.com

Canada
Canadian National Baptist Convention
100 Convention Way
Cochrane, AB T4C 2G2
Canada
Phone: 403-932-5688 (outside Canada); 888-442-2272
Website: www.cnbc.ca

Colorado
Colorado Baptist General Convention
7393 South Alton Way
Centennial, CO 80112-2302
Phone: 303-771-2480
Website: www.saturatecolorado.com

Dakotas
Dakota Baptist Convention
PO Box 549
Rapid City, SD 57709
Phone: 605-716-0130
Website: www.dakotabaptist.com

District of Columbia
District of Columbia Baptist Convention
1628 16th Street NW
Washington, DC 20009
Phone: 202-265-1526
Website: www.dcbaptist.org

Florida
Florida Baptist Convention
6850 Belfort Oaks Place
Jacksonville, FL 32216
Phone: 904-396-2351
Website: www.flbaptist.org

Georgia
Georgia Baptist Mission Board
6405 Sugarloaf Parkway
Duluth, GA 30097-4092
Phone: 800-746-4422
Website: www.gabaptist.org

Hawaii
Hawaii Pacific Baptist Convention
2042 Vancouver Drive
Honolulu, HI 96822
Phone: 808-946-9581
Website: www.hpbaptist.net

Illinois
Illinois Baptist State Association
3085 Stevenson Drive
Springfield, IL 62703
Phone: 217-786-2600
Website: www.ibsa.org

Indiana
State Convention of Baptists in Indiana
7805 State Road 39
Martinsville, IN 46151
Phone: 800-444-5424
Website: www.scbi.org

Iowa
Baptist Convention of Iowa
PO Box 619
Ankeny, IA 50021
Phone: 515-809-2819
Website: www.bciowa.org

Kansas-Nebraska
Kansas Nebraska Convention of Southern Baptists
5410 Southwest Seventh Street
Topeka, KS 66606-2398
Phone: 800-984-9092
Website: www.kncsb.org

Kentucky
Kentucky Baptist Convention
13420 Eastpoint Centre Drive
Louisville, KY 40223
Phone: 800-266-6477
Website: www.kybaptist.org

Louisiana
Louisiana Baptist Convention
PO Box 311
Alexandria, LA 71309
Phone: 318-448-3402
Website: www.louisianabaptists.org

Maryland/Delaware
Baptist Convention of Maryland/Delaware
10255 Old Columbia Road
Columbia, MD 21046
Phone: 800-466-5290
Web site: www.bcmd.org

Michigan
Baptist State Convention of Michigan
8420 Runyan Lake Road
Fenton, MI 48430
Phone: 810-714-1907
Website: www.bscm.org

Minnesota-Wisconsin
Minnesota Wisconsin Baptist Convention
519 16th Street Southeast
Rochester, MN 55904
Phone: 507-282-3636
Website: www.mwbc.org

Mississippi
Mississippi Baptist Convention Board
PO Box 530
Jackson, MS 39205-0530
Phone: 601-968-3800
Website: www.mbcb.org

Missouri
Missouri Baptist Convention
400 East High Street
Jefferson City, MO 65101-3215
Phone: 800-736-6227
Website: www.mobaptist.org

Montana
Montana Southern Baptist Convention
1130 Cerise Road
Billings, MT 59101
Phone: 406-252-7537
Website: www.mtsbc.org

Nevada
Nevada Baptist Convention
406 California Avenue
Reno, NV 89509
Phone: 775-786-0406
Website: www.nbcsbc.org

New England
Baptist Convention of New England
87 Lincoln Street
Northborough, MA 01532
Phone: 508-393-6013
Website: www.bcne.net

New Mexico
The Baptist Convention of New Mexico
PO Box 94485
Albuquerque, NM 87199-4485
Phone: 800-898-8544
Website: www.bcnm.com

New York
Baptist Convention of New York
6538 Baptist Way
East Syracuse, NY 13057
Phone: 315-433-1001
Website: www.bcnysbc.org

North Carolina
Baptist State Convention of North Carolina
205 Convention Drive
Cary, NC 27511
Phone: 800-395-5102
Website: www.ncbaptist.org

Northwest
Northwest Baptist Convention
3200 Northeast 109th Avenue
Vancouver, WA 98682-7749
Phone: 360-882-2100
Website: www.nwbaptist.org

Ohio
The State Convention of Baptists in Ohio
9000 Antares Avenue
Columbus, OH 43240
Phone: 614-601-6789
Website: www.scbo.org

Oklahoma
Baptist General Convention of Oklahoma
3800 North May Avenue
Oklahoma City, OK 73112
Phone: 405-942-3000
Website: www.bgco.org

Pennsylvania-South Jersey
Baptist Resource Network of Pennsylvania
   and South Jersey
4620 Fritchey Street
Harrisburg, PA 17109
Phone: 800-451-6599
Website: www.brnonline.org

South Carolina
South Carolina Baptist Convention
190 Stoneridge Drive
Columbia, SC 29210
Phone: 803-765-0030
Website: www.scbaptist.org

Tennessee
Tennessee Baptist Mission Board
PO Box 682789
Franklin, TN 37068
Phone: 800-558-2090
Website: www.tnbaptist.org

Texas
Baptist General Convention of Texas
7557 Rambler Road, Suite 1200
Dallas, TX 75231-2388
Phone: 888-244-9400
Website: www.texasbaptists.org

Southern Baptists of Texas Convention
PO Box 1988
Grapevine, TX 76099-1988
Phone: 877-953-7282
Website: www.sbtexas.com

Utah-Idaho
Utah-Idaho Southern Baptist Convention
PO Box 1347
Draper, UT 84020-1347
Phone: 801-572-5350
Website: www.uisbc.org

Virginia
Baptist General Association of Virginia
2828 Emerywood Parkway
Henrico, VA 23294
Phone: 800-255-2428
Website: www.bgav.org

Southern Baptist Conservatives of Virginia
4956 Dominion Boulevard
Glen Allen, VA 23060
Phone: 804-270-1848
Website: www.sbcv.org

West Virginia
The West Virginia Convention of Southern Baptists
28 Mission Way
Scott Depot, WV 25560
Phone: 304-757-0944
Website: www.wvcsb.org

Wyoming
Wyoming Southern Baptist Convention
3925 Casper Mountain Road
Casper, WY 82601
Phone: 307-472-4087
Website: www.wyomingsbc.org

PASTOR SEARCH COMMITTEE COVENANT OF AGREEMENTS

As a member of the pastor search committee of _____ Baptist Church,
I gladly covenant to participate in the work of the committee according to the following
agreements.

Covenant of Ethical Behavior

I agree to relate to each member in a manner consistent with the ethical standards
characterized by Jesus Christ.

Covenant of Spiritual Preparation

I agree to make Bible study and prayer ongoing priorities in my life.

Covenant of Prayer

I agree to pray daily for each committee member and for the work of the church.

Covenant of Unity

I agree to work in unity, not regarding myself as of more value than others, "diligently
keeping the unity of the Spirit with the peace that binds us" (Eph. 4:3).

Covenant of Honesty and Openness

I agree to be honest and open with others on the committee, always seeking the Holy
Spirit's guidance so that the fruit of the Spirit identified in Galatians 5:22-23 will
characterize my participation.

Covenant of Confidentiality

I agree to refrain from discussing with persons outside the committee, including members
of my family, information shared in committee meetings unless the committee agrees
to release information to other church members.

Covenant of Faithfulness

I agree to remain faithful to the church and its ministries so that church members will
have confidence in the committee and so that I can effectively and honestly interpret
the work of the church to prospective pastors being considered by the committee.

_____   _____

Signature   Date

PASTOR-CHURCH COVENANT OF RELATIONSHIP

This covenant between _____ (pastor) and _____ Church
at (address) _____
is entered to provide clear understandings about relationships and responsibilities necessary to bring glory to God
through the growth of the church and the pastor throughout the tenure of his ministry.

The church and the pastor are pleased to enter this covenant, effective _____ (date).
This covenant shall continue as long as both the pastor and the church believe it is God's will for them.

Led by the Spirit of God, the pastor agrees to the following.
1. Seek the mind of Christ and the guidance of the Holy Spirit in all things.
2. Be a person of integrity in his family, the church, and the community.
3. Be loving and gracious to all.
4. Be diligent in work according to a work schedule shared with the church.
5. Use his ministry gifts, knowledge, and wisdom to glorify Christ through the church.
6. Provide spiritual leadership to the church.
7. Lead the church in planning and implementing ministries that fulfill the Great Commission.
8. Preach to instruct, inspire, and enable the church for ministry.
9. Coordinate baptismal services, officiate weddings and funerals, or delegate these responsibilities.
10. Mediate conflict to produce healthy, productive relationships in the church.
11. Lead the church staff and delegate responsibilities to staff members or church officers.
12. Lead the church leadership team (church council) in its tasks or delegate responsibility.
13. Counsel other church leaders and ministry teams about their work.
14. Evangelize the lost through preaching and personally as a disciple of Jesus Christ.
15. Care for persons with special needs and lead others to be involved in caring ministries.
16. Respect church members' ministry gifts and encourage members' growth and involvement
    in the life of the church.
17. Represent the church in community and denominational activities.

Led by the Spirit of God, the church agrees to the following.
1. Be loving and gracious to the pastor and his family.
2. Pray for spiritual power in his life and work.
3. Respectfully relate to him as God's anointed leader for this task.
4. Support his leadership with active participation in the church's ministries.
5. Talk with him about personal concerns instead of talking about him to others.
6. Provide resources for doing the work to which he is committed, including competent
    and loyal staff members, as needed.

7. Provide a salary and benefits commensurate with the duties of his office.

8. Free him to do the work to which he is called as other church leaders and members fulfill their responsibilities.

9. Annually provide a fair, impartial, and constructive ministry review.

The church and the pastor agree to the following work schedule.

Inasmuch as the pastor has responsibilities that cannot be measured in definite schedules of time, he will give care to scheduling his time and activities to best serve the Lord and the interests of the church, allowing time for personal and family needs. He is encouraged to have two days off each week while being on call in times of crisis. The pastor and the church will be best served if the pastor establishes a schedule of office hours and informs members of the schedule. The pastor's responsibilities require many hours of isolation for prayer, study, and preparation. Church members will regard this time as vital to the ministry and, whenever possible, arrange for consultation and counsel at other times.

The church and the pastor agree to the following salary, housing, benefits, and expenses (see tool 5 for descriptions).

The church will provide for the pastor as spelled out on the attached checklist (see tool 6):

1. Salary
2. Housing
3. Protection benefits
4. Ministry and continuing-education expenses
5. Vacation, leave, and sabbatical

When the pastor search committee and the pastor agree on the conditions of this covenant of relationship, the committee will recommend that the church adopt the covenant and call the pastor.

This covenant of relationship is entered by:

_____

Pastor

_____

Chairman, Pastor Search Committee

_____

Date

PASTOR'S SALARY, HOUSING, BENEFITS, AND EXPENSES

Work with the appropriate church committees, such as personal, budget, or finance, to provide a budget line item for each of the following expense areas. These figures can show the total budget commitment to the pastor and can distinguish between personal benefits provided for the pastor and the expenses he incurs in providing effective ministry.

Salary

To assist you, many Baptist state conventions (see tool 2) have information from church-related compensation surveys. The pastor's salary should reflect several factors:

1. Investment in educational preparation
2. Years of experience
3. Range of responsibilities, including supervision of staff and volunteers
4. Cost of living
5. Salaries for management positions in the corporate community in which your church is located
6. Salaries of pastors in other churches with comparable responsibilities

Housing

The time between pastors may provide a good opportunity to consider all of the options for providing housing for your pastor.

Some churches provide a church-owned house for the pastor and his family, including the cost of utilities. This arrangement has several benefits. The pastor doesn't have to be concerned about finding a home when he arrives or about selling a home when he leaves. Church members feel pride in owning and maintaining the parsonage. In the short term this approach may be more economical for the church. However, it also has drawbacks. The pastor builds no equity toward future housing, especially for retirement. The family has no guarantee of housing if the pastor dies or becomes disabled. Conflict can arise over lawn maintenance, pets, and responsibility for damage.

Other churches provide a housing allowance to enable the pastor to purchase or rent a house. The housing allowance, combined with the salary, is the equivalent to gross income on a paycheck. The pastor should recommend and the church should approve an amount to be reported as salary and an amount to be reported as housing allowance. The housing allowance, as long as it is within the housing-rental-allowance criteria of the Internal Revenue Service, is not taxable.

When the church already has a house for the pastor, it can consider selling the house to the pastor at its current appraised value and providing a housing allowance to cover the cost of housing payments. Or the church can finance the sale itself so that the principal plus interest is paid back to the church. The pastor benefits by not having to make a high downpayment. When the pastor leaves, the church may agree to buy the house at the appraised value at that time, keeping the property for the church's continuing ministry.

An ordained minister is an employee of the church for income-tax purposes but is self-employed for Social Security purposes. Therefore, the housing allowance is not taxable as income. But the pastor pays both the church's part and his personal part of Social Security taxes. For this reason some churches add a Social Security offset to the salary and housing allowance. The amount, equal to the employer's share of his Social Security, must be reported by the church and the pastor as income.

Protection Benefits

These benefits should be considered over and above the basic salary and housing allowance. They provide for the pastor and his family in the event of medical needs, death, disability, or retirement. Some suggestions follow.

1. Provide health and medical insurance to cover some or all of the costs of doctor visits, hospitalization, medications, and dental and vision coverage. If the medical plan does not cover the cost of an annual physical, include that cost.
2. Determine the number of days for sick leave. Provide expenses and honoraria for those who substitute for the pastor.
3. Provide life insurance valued at least four times the pastor's salary and housing, plus coverage for his wife and children. Coverage could be half that of the pastor for the wife and $5,000 for each dependent. These insurance premiums are taxable income. The church may also consider $50,000 term life-insurance coverage as a tax-sheltered benefit.
4. Offer disability insurance to provide income during the pastor's waiting period for Social Security coverage if he becomes disabled and is unable to serve the church.
5. Provide a retirement annuity through the Annuity Board of the Southern Baptist Convention to ensure that the pastor will have income to meet the needs of his family during normal retirement years. Without an adequate retirement annuity, a pastor will be tempted to continue in the pastoral role late in life when failing energy and health may limit his effectiveness in ministry. Contact the Annuity Board representative in your Baptist state convention (see tool 2).
6. Some churches also provide a 401(k) savings plan for the pastor.

Ministry Expenses

These expenses result from the pastor's ministry. Examples include the following.
1. If the pastor uses his personal car for church business, provide a mileage-allowance reimbursement. The best guide is the allowance approved by the Internal Revenue Service.
2. Provide an allowance for the pastor to buy books and media resources for use in study for preaching and ministry responsibilities.

3. Provide an allowance for the pastor's use when he entertains guests of the church.
4. Provide for costs when he represents the church in meetings of the association and state convention.

Continuing-Education Expenses

In a fast-changing world, much of what is learned in educational institutions becomes out-of-date very quickly. Although the truth of the gospel never changes, the world in which the gospel is preached and practiced changes constantly. If a pastor hasn't participated in continuing-education experiences in three years, he is not keeping up with the understandings and resources that are vital to church ministry. Many churches provide money for the pastor to participate in continuing-education activities. These can include conferences, seminars, and Internet-delivered seminary and graduate-school courses. Costs include registration fees, materials, and textbooks. Sometimes travel, housing, and meals are also provided.

Vacation

Determine how many weeks of vacation the church will provide the pastor each year. This determination can be based on years of experience and the amount of vacation the prospective pastor currently receives. Include in the agreement that the church will pay for a substitute preacher's expenses and honorarium.

Leave

Provide a specified number of days or weeks that the pastor can be away from the church to lead revivals, conferences, or other events. Include in the agreement that the church will pay for a substitute preacher's expenses and honorarium.

Sabbatical

Some churches provide a sabbatical of a few months after a certain number of years of service. Included in this benefit are any costs for substitute preachers' expenses and honoraria.

CHECKLIST FOR PASTOR'S SALARY, HOUSING, BENEFITS, AND EXPENSES

Salary

		YES	NO

1. Monthly salary will begin at $ _____ .

   Dates of month salary will be paid: _____

2. Schedule for review and consideration of increase: _____

3. Will church provide Social Security offset?   ❑   ❑

Housing

4. Will church provide housing for pastor and family?   ❑   ❑

   If yes, in what form?   ❑ Parsonage   ❑ Allowance: $_____ monthly

5. Will church provide utilities or allowance? If allowance, amount: $_____   ❑   ❑

   Electricity: $_____   ❑   ❑

   Phone: $_____   ❑   ❑

   Water: $_____   ❑   ❑

   Other: $_____   ❑   ❑

6. Will church assist pastor in purchasing home?   ❑   ❑

   If yes, indicate the following.

   Will provide downpayment as a gift in the amount of $_____ or as a loan

   in the amount of $_____ at an interest rate of _____ percent to be repaid

   at $_____ monthly. Amount to be paid in full within _____ days of termination

   as pastor.

Protection Benefits

7. Will church provide the following insurance coverage? If yes, describe coverage.

   Health: $_____ _____   ❑   ❑

   Dental: $_____ _____   ❑   ❑

   Vision: $_____ _____   ❑   ❑

   Life: $_____ _____   ❑   ❑

   Disability: $_____ _____   ❑   ❑

	YES	NO

8. Will church provide time off for illness?   ❑   ❑

   If yes, amount of time annually: _____

9. Will church pay salary and benefits during illness?   ❑   ❑

   For how long? _____

10. Will church provide honorarium and expenses for pulpit supply when pastor is ill?   ❑   ❑

    For how long? _____

11. Will church provide annual physical examination for pastor?   ❑   ❑

12. Will church provide retirement plan for pastor?   ❑   ❑

    If yes, amount: $_____

13. Will church provide a 401(k) savings plan for pastor?   ❑   ❑

    If yes, amount: $_____

Ministry and Continuing-Education Expenses

14. Will a church-owned automobile be provided for business travel?   ❑   ❑

15. Will monthly car reimbursement be provided?   ❑   ❑

    If yes, in the amount of $_____ per month or

    _____ cents per mile for travel on church business

16. Will church provide entertainment expenses?   ❑   ❑

    If yes, amount per month: $_____ or reimbursement: $_____

17. Will church provide annual allowance for book and media resources?   ❑   ❑

    If yes, annual amount: $_____

18. Will time off be provided for study leave and training conferences?   ❑   ❑

    If yes, how much time annually? _____

19. Will church pay cost of job-related training?   ❑   ❑

    If yes, how much of total cost? $_____

Vacation, Leave, Sabbatical

20. Church will provide _____ days off each week.

21. Will church provide annual, paid vacation?   ❑   ❑

    If yes, number of weeks: _____ first year,

    _____ second year, and _____ thereafter.

    Can vacation be accumulated if unused?   ❑   ❑

    Will church provide honorarium and expenses for pulpit supply?   ❑   ❑

	YES	NO

22. Will church provide time off for bereavement? ❑ ❑

If yes, how much time? _____

Will church provide honorarium and expenses for pulpit supply? ❑ ❑

23. Will church provide time off for revivals? ❑ ❑

If yes, how much time? _____

Will church provide honorarium and expenses for pulpit supply? ❑ ❑

24. Will church provide time off for conferences and retreats? ❑ ❑

If yes, how much time? _____

Will church provide honorarium and expenses for pulpit supply? ❑ ❑

25. Will church provide time off for—

• annual state evangelism conference? ❑ ❑

• annual associational meeting? ❑ ❑

• annual state convention? ❑ ❑

• annual Southern Baptist Convention? ❑ ❑

If yes, how much time? _____

Will church provide honorarium and expenses for pulpit supply? ❑ ❑

Will expenses be paid? ❑ ❑

Will wife's expenses be paid? ❑ ❑

Other

26. Will church provide all moving expenses? ❑ ❑

27. _____

28. _____

29. _____

30. _____

PASTOR SEARCH CONGREGATIONAL SURVEY

Your Expectations

Please answer the following questions to indicate your expectations for our church's next pastor.

1. What is the desired age range for the pastor? Check one.
   - ❑ Under 20
   - ❑ 30–39
   - ❑ 50–59
   - ❑ No age preference
   - ❑ 20–29
   - ❑ 40–49
   - ❑ 60 or more

2. What is the minimum acceptable educational level you expect the pastor to have attained? Check one.
   - ❑ Less than high-school graduate
   - ❑ High-school graduate only
   - ❑ Some college or professional school
   - ❑ College graduate (bachelor's degree)
   - ❑ Attended seminary
   - ❑ Master's degree from seminary
   - ❑ Doctoral degree from seminary
   - ❑ Formal education degree not important

3. What are acceptable marital statuses for the prospective pastor? Check all that apply.
   - ❑ Never married
   - ❑ Separated or divorced
   - ❑ Currently married
   - ❑ Widowed

4. What pastoral or professional ministry experience should be required? Check one.
   - ❑ No prior experience necessary
   - ❑ 1–5 years of prior experience as pastor
   - ❑ 1–5 years of prior church-ministry experience (such as church staff)
   - ❑ 6–10 years of prior experience as pastor
   - ❑ 6–10 years of prior church-ministry experience (such as church staff)
   - ❑ More than 10 years of prior experience as pastor
   - ❑ More than 10 years of prior church-ministry experience (such as church staff)

5. What should the size of the prospective pastor's current church be in relation to our church? Check one.
   - ❑ Much smaller than our church
   - ❑ Somewhat smaller than our church
   - ❑ About the same size as our church
   - ❑ Somewhat larger than our church
   - ❑ Much larger than our church
   - ❑ Doesn't matter

6. Which two of the following do you consider the most important strengths needed by the incoming pastor? Check only two.
   - ❑ Preaching
   - ❑ Administration
   - ❑ Leadership
   - ❑ Relationships

7. The following are activities to which a pastor may allocate time each week. Read all choices and check the three areas that should be the top time priorities of our new pastor. Check only three.

❑ Administration, including tasks related to the church office, finances, and facility

❑ Correspondence with members by phone, email, and other electronic means

❑ Counseling individuals with personal and spiritual problems

❑ Visiting members in the hospital and in nursing homes

❑ Visiting members or prospects at home or over a meal

❑ Sermon preparation

❑ Prayer

❑ Attending social gatherings and special events of ministries, classes, and groups in the church

❑ Planning and organizing ministry activities

❑ Meeting with ministry leaders who plan and organize ministry activities

8. Compared to our church's current worship services, would you want the prospective pastor to lead in making any of the following changes? Check one.

❑ Include more traditional musical elements (classical hymns, older praise songs, fewer instruments).

❑ Include more contemporary musical elements (newer praise songs, upbeat arrangements, contemporary instruments).

❑ Use the same musical style as today.

9. Which of the following elements of preaching style effectively communicate God's Word to you? Check all that apply.

❑ Logical, detailed, point by point

❑ Personal, relational, engaging

❑ Textual (the Scripture text provides the meaning)

❑ Narrative (use of stories to illustrate points)

❑ Sermon series (spending multiple weeks on a topic)

❑ Bible book (spending multiple weeks on a Bible book)

❑ Challenging, appealing for action or change

10. Of the ministry priorities in our church, which three of the following does the incoming pastor need to emphasize most? Check only three.[1]

❑ Discipleship and spiritual formation

❑ Developing small Bible study groups/classes

❑ Building relationships in which people are connected and care for one another

❑ Evangelism and showing Jesus through word and action

❑ Leadership vision and a compelling plan for the future of the church

❑ Care for the poor (social compassion)

❑ Denominational emphases, programs, and giving

❑ Missions involvement and giving

❑ Prayer

❑ Organizing ministries and empowering leaders for ministry

❑ Understanding the context of our local community and approaching it with a missionary mentality

❑ Corporate and personal worship

❑ Strengthening families

About You

11. What is your gender?

❑ Male   ❑ Female

12. What is your current age?

❑ Under 12   ❑ 30–39   ❑ 60–69

❑ 12–17   ❑ 40–49   ❑ 70 or more

❑ 18–29   ❑ 50–59

13. What is your marital status? Check all that apply.

❑ Never married   ❑ Separated or divorced

❑ Currently married   ❑ Widowed

14. Do you have children under 18 living at home?

❑ Yes   ❑ No

15. Circle the number that best describes your participation in the activities of this church.

Not very active   **Very active**

1   2   3   4   5

1. LifeWay Christian Resources has two assessment tools that go deeper on topics introduced in question 10. Transformational Church Assessment Tool (*www.transformationalchurch.com*) measures the health of your church. Transformational Discipleship Assessment (*tda.lifeway.com*) measures the spiritual formation and maturity of your congregation.

To purchase and download a more comprehensive congregational survey or for additional versions for other staff members, visit *www.lifewayresearch.com*.

TOOL 8

POSITION INSIGHTS AND LEADING FROM YOUR STRENGTHS PROFILES

Finding the pastor God has for your church can be a difficult, consuming process. Using Position Insights Profile™ and Leading from Your Strengths Profile™ can provide a unique, comprehensive process for finding the right pastor for your church. The step-by-step assessment process follows, along with ideas for getting the best insights and results during and after the selection process. The two main questions these assessments can help you answer are:

1. What are the main expectations and behavioral profile for the pastor of our church?
2. Who will best fit the profile of the position, based on his dominant and natural strengths?

Every work environment requires a mix of human behavior to accomplish its goals. Each person brings certain personal strengths to his or her position. Pastors can best serve their organizations by being matched with their position. When you match a pastor's God-given strengths with the position, he will be better able to perform the tasks of the position. If he is required to continually perform work that does not match his natural strengths, the pastor will experience tension or stress, resulting in tension or stress in the congregation.

The Position Insights process was developed to assess the unique strengths and behavior that are needed to successfully complete a particular position's responsibilities. This process allows your committee to identify the behavioral demands of the position itself, not the behavior of a pastor in the position. Therefore, responses to this instrument must objectively focus on the position. If the position could talk, this is the way it would rank the statements in each group.

Four essential factors are at work in the position of pastor and in every candidate you consider. The role of pastor demands from a person a certain degree of each one of these factors:

1. Solving problems
2. Influencing others
3. Responding to the pace of the environment
4. Following rules and procedures

Predictable conflicts can be avoided if the pastor search committee assesses how much strength or intensity of each one of these factors is needed for someone to be effective as the pastor of your church. To ensure a smooth selection process with Position Insights Profile and Leading from Your Strengths Profile, remember these key points.

1. It's important to get a clear picture of the extent to which these behavioral factors are evident in each candidate.
2. Different types of people respond much differently to the same issue or problem.
3. Knowing what the position demands in each of these four areas will help you determine the best candidate.
4. Together Position Insights Profile and Leading from Your Strengths Profile give a clear picture of the intensity of each factor in a position and in a candidate.

Selecting the best candidate because you think that he is well rounded and has impressive credentials may sound like a good plan, but using these criteria can actually increase the turnover of pastors. Consider these reasons.

1. Finding a great person with lots of ability and potential to excel as pastor is appealing and comforting. But thinking you can make a good person fit any position is flawed reasoning.

2. A multitalented, well-rounded person may be able to learn to do anything and fit into many different types of roles. But this person's satisfaction will eventually begin to wane because the longer a person regularly tries to be all things to all people, the more he will acccumulate internal frustration and related stress. It's the "square peg in a round hole" scenario.

3. A pastor who is not matched to the specific behavioral demands of the position will undoubtedly become frustrated and prove to be less than ideal in a short time.

4. It is crucial that the strengths and behavioral style of your top candidates be matched with the expectations for the position. This is where Position Insights Profile and Leading from Your Strengths Profile can help. With Position Insights Profile the pastor search committee will be able to get a clear picture of the behavioral demands of the position. With Leading from Your Strengths Profile your committee can obtain a profile of each candidate and can compare the position profile with each candidate's profile. This assessment will give insights on how each candidate solves problems, influences others, responds to the pace of work, and follows rules and procedures.

The Position Insights process, outlined below, will help your committee accurately assess and identify the behavioral demands of the desired pastor in your church. It should be used in conjunction with other information, such as experience and education, to form a comprehensive view of a candidate. If the process outline is followed, it will accomplish these important objectives:

1. Position Insights creates a strong consensus and understanding among committee members about the expectations for the position.

2. The process provides a clear understanding and outline of the personal strengths needed to be an effective pastor of your church.

Refer to *www.ministryinsights.com* for additional information and related online resources. It is your beginning point for the four-step process below. Overview all steps before beginning with step 1.

Step 1

For the Position Insights process it is recommended that the pastor search committee complete the preassessment exercises below. These are designed to help build teamwork, understanding, and closeness in order to eliminate possible misunderstandings and biases during and after the selection process. However, step 1 is not a requirement for a successful Position Insights Profile. You can purchase the appropriate number of Leading from Your Strengths Profile at *www.ministryinsights.com*. You will be emailed the unique password links to give to each committee member.

1. All pastor search committee members should individually complete Leading from Your Strengths Profile before starting the Position Insights process.

2. Each committee member should share his Leading from Your Strengths report with the group. This will enable members to better understand one another and to become more familiar with the material in the Position Insights Profile Report.

3. Committee members should set a time to complete the Position Insights process together and to familiarize themselves with the demands of the position in question before starting the process.

Step 2

1. Because each person on the pastor search committee needs a copy of Position Insights Profile Response Form at the end of this tool, print the 14-item survey for each committee member.

2. There are 14 categories, each with 4 items to be considered. Have each committee member complete the survey. This is not a timed response, but please take only the time needed to complete this form. Indicate your choices as follows: for the most important statement to the position of pastor, enter 1; for the second most important statement, enter 2; and so forth. Within each group, each number (1–4) must be used only once, and every box must have a number in it.

3. Reach a consensus. As a committee, rank each of the 4 statements in the 14 groups in order of importance or relevance to the position of pastor in your church. Each block requires agreement by the entire group on the order of importance of each statement before moving to the next block. If the position could talk, what would it say?

4. Purchase your Position Insights Profile at *www.ministryinsights.com.* Because the search committee has developed a consensus response, select Position Insights Group. You will immediately be emailed a link to enter your data.

5. To score the instrument, use the emailed link to go to the Position Insights online form. Follow the simple on-screen instructions for transferring your written data to the online form.

6. Position Insights Report will immediately be generated and emailed.

7. Print Position Insights Report, using Adobe Acrobat Reader.

8. Take time in a committee meeting to discuss the report. It is important that everyone agree on the position profile.

Step 3

1. Purchase the appropriate number of Leading from Your Strengths Profile at *www.ministryinsights.com.* You will be emailed the unique password links to give to your candidates.

2. Ask your top candidates to take Leading from Your Strengths Profile. Have the reports sent to the committee.

3. As a committee, compare each candidate's Leading from Your Strengths Profile to the Position Insights Profile.

4. Compare each candidate's Core Style Graph in his Leading from Your Strengths Report and determine its similarity to the Position Insights Graph. A close Core Style Graph match indicates that the candidate's core style is compatible with the position requirements.

5. Discuss differences among the top candidates' profiles and the profile of the position.

6. Decide how closely a candidate's profile needs to match the Position Insights Profile to continue being considered.

7. Reach an agreement on the best match for the position.

Step 4

1. Follow up with the prospective pastor during the interview.

2. Review the Position Insights Profile and his Leading from Your Strengths Report to discuss the expectations and demands of the position of pastor in your church.

POSITION INSIGHTS PROFILE
RESPONSE FORM

This position calls for:

1
- ❑ A. Analysis of data and facts before acting
- ❑ B. Tactful decisions
- ❑ C. Quick and forceful decisions
- ❑ D. Logical thinking before making decisions

2
- ❑ A. Few changes
- ❑ B. Some changes
- ❑ C. Many changes
- ❑ D. No change

3
- ❑ A. Clean, tidy, and organized workstation
- ❑ B. Freedom to act independently
- ❑ C. Consistent performance
- ❑ D. Conveying confidence in others

4
- ❑ A. Work to be completed accurately the first time
- ❑ B. Being flexible
- ❑ C. Planning ahead on a large scale
- ❑ D. Identification with the team

5
- ❑ A. A systematic way to do things
- ❑ B. Contact with many people
- ❑ C. Making quick decisions
- ❑ D. Being diplomatic and cooperative

6
- ❑ A. Avoiding trouble
- ❑ B. Solving problems
- ❑ C. Verbalizing thoughts and ideas
- ❑ D. Working with things

7
- ❑ A. Staying at one workstation
- ❑ B. Expediting action
- ❑ C. Adhering to procedures
- ❑ D. Generating enthusiasm

8
- ❑ A. Influencing others to a common goal
- ❑ B. Concentrating on details
- ❑ C. Challenging assignments
- ❑ D. Exhibiting patience

9
- ❑ A. Contacting people
- ❑ B. Following directions
- ❑ C. Getting results
- ❑ D. Performing to standards

10
- ❑ A. Following procedures to perfection
- ❑ B. Solving people problems
- ❑ C. Bold, aggressive actions
- ❑ D. Routine work

11
- ❑ A. High quality controls
- ❑ B. Creative and original thinking
- ❑ C. Optimistic outlook
- ❑ D. Working with the system

12
- ❑ A. Complete authority to carry out responsibilities
- ❑ B. Analysis of facts and data
- ❑ C. Many people interactions
- ❑ D. Patience

13
- ❑ A. Freedom from excessive detailed work
- ❑ B. Task-oriented concentration
- ❑ C. Balanced judgment
- ❑ D. Friendly work environment

14
- ❑ A. More emphasis on quality than efficiency
- ❑ B. Freedom from conflict and confrontation
- ❑ C. Highly persuasive communications
- ❑ D. Accepting and initiating change

DEMOGRAPHIC PROFILE OF CHURCH MEMBERSHIP

Please complete one form per family. Answer with check marks or numbers as appropriate.

Check your role in this family: ❑ Husband ❑ Wife ❑ Single ❑ Son ❑ Daughter

1. Family Composition by Gender

_____ Number of males _____ Number of females

2. Family Composition by Ethnic Group

List those relevant for your church, such as Caucasian, African-American, Hispanic, Asian, Native American, etc. Also indicate the number in your family.

_____ _____ _____ _____

_____ _____ _____ _____

_____ _____ _____ _____

3. Age

Write the number of family members in each age bracket.

_____	Birth–5 years	_____	30–39 years
_____	6–11 years	_____	40–49 years
_____	12–17 years	_____	50–59 years
_____	18–29 years	_____	60 or more years

4. Occupations

Write the number of family members in each category.

_____ Clerical (bank teller, bookkeeper, cashier, postal clerk, secretary, typist, etc.)

_____ Craftsman (baker, carpenter, foreman, machinist, mechanic, repairman, etc.)

_____ Farm worker

_____ Homemaker

_____ Laborer (construction worker, freight handler, warehouseman)

_____ Manager (administrator, bank officer, business director, self-employed, etc.)

_____ Operative or transport (assembler, bus driver, inspector, packer, butcher, garage worker, truck driver, etc.)

_____ Professional (accountant, artist, medical professional, engineer, lawyer, minister, scientist, teacher, technician, engineer, etc.)

_____ Sales (advertiser, clerk, insurance agent, sales worker, underwriter, etc.)

_____ Service worker (barber, child care, food service, health worker, policeman, private household cleaning, teacher's aide, etc.)

_____ Part-time employment

_____ Retired

_____ Unemployed

_____ Other: _____

5. Number of Adult Family Members in Home by Marital Status

_____ Single _____ Separated _____ Widowed

_____ Married _____ Divorced

6. **Education Level**

Write the number of family members for whom the category represents the highest education level.

_____ Preschooler at home	_____ Trade or technical school
_____ Kindergarten	_____ Junior college
_____ Elementary school	_____ College
_____ Middle school	_____ Postgraduate work
_____ High school	

7. **Length of Time Each Family Member Has Been a Christian**

Write the number of family members in each category.

_____ Not a Christian	_____ 6–9 years
_____ Less than one year	_____ 10–19 years
_____ 1–2 years	_____ 20–29 years
_____ 3–5 years	_____ 30 or more years

8. **Length of Time Each Family Member Has Been a Member of This Church**

Write the number of family members in each category.

_____ Not a member	_____ 6–9 years
_____ Less than one year	_____ 10–19 years
_____ 1–2 years	_____ 20–29 years
_____ 3–5 years	_____ 30 or more years

9. **Church Attendance**

In a typical four-Sunday month, how often does someone from your family attend the following activities?

_____ Sunday School	_____ Prayer meeting
_____ Morning worship	_____ Church visitation
_____ Discipleship Training	_____ Missions organizations
_____ Evening worship	_____ Age-group activities

10. **Type of Home**

❏ Single-family house
❏ Apartment/condominium with 2–4 units
❏ Apartment/condominium with 5–49 units
❏ Apartment/condominium with 50 or more units
❏ Mobile home/manufactured housing

11. **Length of Time Your Family Has Lived at Present Address**

❏ Fewer than 2 years	❏ 10–19 years
❏ 2–5 years	❏ 20–29 years
❏ 6–9 years	❏ 30 or more years

12. **Approximate Distance You Live from Church Building**

❏ Less than 1 mile	❏ 6–9 miles
❏ 1–3 miles	❏ 10–19 miles
❏ 4–5 miles	❏ 20 or more miles

13. **Locations of Family Births**

_____ Number of family members born in this state
_____ Number of family members born in this community

TOOL 10

DIRECTORY OF SOUTHERN BAPTIST SEMINARIES

Gateway Seminary
3210 East Guasti Road
Ontario, CA 91761-8642
Phone: 909-687-1800
Website: www.gs.edu

Midwestern Baptist Theological Seminary
5001 North Oak Trafficway
Kansas City, MO 64118
Phone: 800-944-6287
Website: www.mbts.edu

New Orleans Baptist Theological Seminary
3939 Gentilly Boulevard
New Orleans, LA 70126
Phone: 800-662-8701
Website: www.nobts.edu

Southeastern Baptist Theological Seminary
120 South Wingate Street
Wake Forest, NC 27587
Phone: 919-761-2100
Website: www.sebts.edu

The Southern Baptist Theological Seminary
2825 Lexington Road
Louisville, KY 40280
Phone: 800-626-5525
Website: www.sbts.edu

Southwestern Baptist Theological Seminary
2001 West Seminary Drive
Fort Worth, TX 76115
Phone: 817-923-1921
Website: www.swbts.edu

Canadian Southern Baptist Seminary
200 Seminary View
Cochrane, Alberta T4C 2G1
Canada
Phone: 403-932-6622
Website: www.csbs.edu

BIOGRAPHICAL PROFILE

Please attach a recent photo.

Name: _____

Home address: _____

_____

Social Security number: _____

Home telephone: _____ **Email:** _____

Age: _____ **Date of birth:** _____ **Birthplace:** _____

Marital status: ❑ Married ❑ Married (previously divorced)

❑ Single (never married) ❑ Single (previously married)

Wife's name: _____

Wife's hometown: _____

Children

Name	Age	Living at home?
_____	____	❑ Yes ❑ No
_____	____	❑ Yes ❑ No
_____	____	❑ Yes ❑ No
_____	____	❑ Yes ❑ No
_____	____	❑ Yes ❑ No
_____	____	❑ Yes ❑ No

Formal Education

High school: _____ Graduation year: _____

City and state: _____

College: _____ Year: ____ Degree: _____

City and state: _____

Seminary: _____ Year: ____ Degree: _____

City and state: _____

Other: _____

Are you presently attending school? ❑ Yes ❑ No

If yes, name of school: _____

City and state: _____

Continuing Education

Include seminars, workshops, seminary programs, etc.

_____
_____
_____

Licensed? ❑ Yes ❑ No Year: _____ By what church? _____

City and state: _____

Ordained? ❑ Yes ❑ No Year: _____ By what church? _____

City and state: _____

Philosophy of Ministry

_____
_____
_____
_____
_____

Experience

Record employment in church-related ministry.

Years	Church/Organization	Location	Attendance	Position
_____ to _____				
_____ to _____				
_____ to _____				
_____ to _____				
_____ to _____				
_____ to _____				
_____ to _____				

Current Church Ministry

Average Sunday School attendance: _____   Average morning worship: _____

Average annual baptisms: _____   Average transfers of membership: _____

Describe the church setting (rural/suburban/urban, growing/declining community, ethnic makeup, etc.).

_____
_____
_____

What has God done during your ministry? _____
_____
_____

Other Current Employment if Bivocational

Company: _____   Telephone: _____

Address:_____

Position: _____   Hours per week: _____

Denominational Service
Include major positions held, writings, teaching assignments for conference centers and retreats, etc.

_____

_____

Civic/Community Activities

_____

_____

Business and/or Military Experience

_____

_____

Hobbies and/or Other Special Interests and Abilities

_____

_____

_____

Other

_____

_____

_____

Church-Related References
1. _____ Telephone: _____
   Address:_____
2. _____ Telephone: _____
   Address:_____
3. _____ Telephone: _____
   Address:_____
4. _____ Telephone: _____
   Address:_____

Character References
1. _____ Telephone: _____
   Address:_____
2. _____ Telephone: _____
   Address:_____
3. _____ Telephone: _____
   Address:_____
4. _____ Telephone: _____
   Address:_____

TOOL 12

PROSPECTIVE-PASTOR EVALUATION

Name: _____ **Initial contact date:** _____

Source of application: _____

Application materials received:

❏ Cover letter   ❏ Letters of reference

❏ Biographical profile   ❏ Background checks

❏ Audiotape/videotape   ❏ Other:

❏ Degree verification

Priority areas (see pp. 29–30):   **Comments**

Philosophy of ministry: _____

Experience: _____

Tenure: _____

Education: _____

Family background: _____

Other interests: _____

Initial evaluations: ❏ Look closer   ❏ Maybe   ❏ Doubtful   ❏ Comments

Actions (date and name of person completing the action):

Sent information: _____

Acknowledged profile: _____

Placed on short list: _____

No further interest: _____

Email: _____

Notes:

_____

_____

_____

_____

_____

_____

_____

DEGREES RELATED TO PASTORAL MINISTRY

Through the years Southern Baptist churches have not required levels of education for ordination. However, preparation for effective ministry requires a balance of intellectual, spiritual, and emotional growth. Therefore, an emphasis on academic preparation for ministry is appropriate.

The following information will help the search committee understand more about educational degrees most often held by persons in pastoral ministry. Not all degree programs offered by Baptist seminaries are included here. The ones listed include the degrees most often listed on the biographical profiles of Baptist pastors.

Degree Terminology

Associate of Divinity (ADiv)
or Diploma in Theology (DipTh)
Requirement: two years of full-time study for someone who is 30 years of age or older without a college degree

Bachelor of Divinity (BD)
or Master of Divinity (MDiv)
Requirement: a college degree plus three years of seminary training. The MDiv has replaced the BD in Baptist seminaries.

Master of Theology (ThM) or Master of Systematic Theology (STM)
Requirement: a college degree, an MDiv, and one additional year of graduate work

Doctor of Ministry (DMin)
Requirement: a college degree, an MDiv, and a minimum of one year of graduate work emphasizing practical aspects of pastoral ministry, plus a written project

Doctor of Theology (ThD),
Doctor of Sacred Theology (STD),
or Doctor of Philosophy (PhD)
These degrees are primarily earned by those intending to teach in colleges, universities, or seminaries. However, some pastors earn these degrees. Requirement: a college degree, an MDiv, and a minimum of two years of graduate work, plus a written academic thesis

Honorary Degrees

Most honorary degrees are conferred to recognize outstanding service rather than academic achievement. The most familiar of these is the Doctor of Divinity (DD). The value of the degree varies according to the integrity and excellence of the institution conferring the degree.

Certificates and Diplomas

Many pastors respond to God's call at a time in life when age, family responsibility, financial considerations, and other factors make it unreasonably difficult to secure a basic college degree as a prerequisite for seminary study. Often they bring to ministry a background in business, industry, or military life that may help compensate for the lack of a college or seminary degree. These individuals may enroll in seminary courses designed especially for them.

Seminary Extension of the six Southern Baptist seminaries offers a variety of biblical, theological, and practical courses at extension centers and by independent study using CD-ROMs or the Internet. Basic Bible-study courses lead to certificates. Courses leading to seminary-extension diplomas are available for those with high-school through seminary educational background.

CONFIDENTIAL PERSONNEL INFORMATION

The contents of this file are confidential personnel information. This information was gathered solely to help the pastor search committee make informed decisions about recommending this person to a position of ministry.

Using this information for any other purposes is a violation of confidentiality and personal privacy. Violating this purpose may result in significant legal repercussions.

The information in this file is for use only by the pastor search committee in determining a person's suitability to serve as the pastor of _____ Baptist Church and cannot be used for any other reason.

TOOL 15

REFERENCE RELEASE

I hereby authorize _____ Baptist Church of _____ to verify all information contained in my application or other written communications, including information from all former churches in which I have served as a pastor, been a member, or been ordained.

I recognize that this verification process will include confidential contacts with former church officers, members, pastoral colleagues, associational and state-convention personnel, colleges, universities, and seminaries, as well as other business and professional references.

I further authorize that any personnel at former places of employment, churches, or references may disclose any and all information about my work history, personal characteristics, salary, work habits, or other areas of importance to this organization.

Furthermore, I waive the right to take legal action against the aforementioned churches, their members and officers, or references for releasing such requested information.

I understand this authorization form and agree to the release and verification of the aforementioned information.

_____   _____

Signature   Date

PORTFOLIO OF CHURCH AND COMMUNITY

Church Items

1. Profile of the prospective pastor
2. Profile of the church
3. Mission and/or vision statements
4. Strategic planning documents
5. Constitution and bylaws
6. History
7. Annual Church Profile
8. Copies of recent Sunday bulletins
9. Copies of recent church newsletters
10. Pictorial directory
11. Current budget
12. List of all officers
13. List of all organizational leaders
14. Pictures of the property
15. Other items the committee chooses to include

Local Baptist-Association Items

1. Associational annual report
2. Recent copy of the associational newsletter
3. Associational history (if available)
4. Biographical sketch of the director of associational missions
5. Other items the committee chooses to include

Community Items

1. Profile of the community
2. Maps of the community, city, county, and state where the church is located
3. Information about schools
4. Information about homes for sale in the area of the church
5. Socioeconomic, ethnic, and other demographics of the area served by the church (not included in item 1)
6. Chamber of commerce promotional material
7. Other items the committee chooses to include

LETTER FOR WRITTEN REFERENCES

Using church letterhead, send this letter to each reference with the pastor's "Reference Release" (tool 15); "Character-Reference Inquiry" (tool 18); and a stamped, addressed envelope.

Today's date

Formal heading

Dear _____:

_____ has given us your name as a reference.

Our pastor search committee is currently exploring the possibility of _____ coming to serve our church as pastor. As a part of our background screening, he signed a release form giving permission for references to share information about him. You will find enclosed a photocopy of the signed release form.

Please help us understand how the qualifications of this prospective pastor might meet the needs of our church by filling out the enclosed character-reference inquiry and returning it to us as quickly as possible. A stamped, addressed envelope is provided for your convenience.

Please pray for our committee as we continue our search process. We will depend on your help in protecting the candidate's present ministry by not telling anyone about this inquiry.

Sincerely,

_____

Chairman or Secretary, Pastor Search Committee

Enclosures

CHARACTER-REFERENCE INQUIRY

Name of prospective pastor: _____

The person named above has been recommended to us for the position of pastor. Please supply the information requested below and any additional comments that might give us a picture of his character. Information will be kept confidential.

1. How long have you known the prospect? _____

2. In what capacity have you known the pastor? (Member/leader in church, colleague in ministry, coministry role in church, business associate, etc.)

    _____

    _____

3. Please rate the prospect by checking the appropriate box beside each qualification. We aren't expecting perfection, so be straightforward.

Qualification	Excellent	Good	Fair	Poor
Creativity				
Work attitude				
Ability to get along with others				
Cooperation				
Dependability				
Honesty				
Personal habits				
Emotional maturity				
Sense of humor				
Initiative				
Perseverance				
Openness to others' ideas				
Care for people				
Flexibility				
Preaching				
Teaching				
Problem solving				
Keeping confidences				
Financial responsibility				

4. What evidence can you give that he is a committed, growing Christian? _____

_____

_____

5. What is the greatest interest or the major emphasis of his ministry? _____

_____

_____

6. What are his greatest strengths? _____

_____

_____

7. Are you aware of reasons he might be open to a new ministry? ❑ Yes ❑ No
   If yes, what reasons? _____

_____

_____

8. Do you have any information that would cause you to have reservations about his appropriateness
   for pastoral ministry? ❑ Yes ❑ No
   If yes, what? _____

_____

_____

9. Have you had any personal experience that would lead you to question his integrity, honesty, ethics,
   or conduct? ❑ Yes ❑ No
   If yes, what? _____

_____

_____

10. Do you know whether this person has ever left a job or ministry position because of charges or accusations
    related to conduct or beliefs? ❑ Yes ❑ No
    If yes, what do you know of the circumstances? _____

_____

_____

11. Would you positively recommend him for ministry at our church? ❑ Yes ❑ No
    Why or why not? _____

_____

_____

12. Have any questions been raised about his personal finances or handling of church funds? ❏ Yes ❏ No
    If yes, what questions? _____
    _____
    _____

13. Are you aware of any reports of sexual misconduct? ❏ Yes ❏ No
    If yes, what were those reports? _____
    _____
    _____

14. Based on your knowledge and his reputation, is his marriage healthy and stable? ❏ Yes ❏ No
    Explain: _____
    _____
    _____

15. Do you have any confidential information you do not feel free to reveal to us about his fitness for ministry?
    ❏ Yes ❏ No

16. Please provide the names, phone numbers, and/or addresses of other persons who have worked closely with him or are otherwise well acquainted with him and would be helpful references for our church in assessing the candidate's character.
    _____
    _____

Additional comments:
_____
_____
_____
_____
_____

_____   _____
Signature   Date

Please return this form to:
_____, Chairman, Pastor Search Committee
_____ Baptist Church

_____
Address

_____
City, state, ZIP

LETTER FOR TELEPHONE INTERVIEWS

Using church letterhead, send this letter to each reference with the pastor's "Reference Release" (tool 15).

Today's date

Formal heading

Dear _____:

Your name has been given by _____ as a reference.

Our pastor search committee is currently exploring the possibility of _____ coming to serve our church as pastor. As a part of our background screening, he signed a release form giving permission for references to share information about him. You will find enclosed a photocopy of the signed release form.

To save you time, we have asked _____, who is a member of our search committee, to call you on the telephone and ask you a number of questions. I hope this will meet with your approval.

Please pray for our committee as we continue our search process. We will depend on your help in protecting the candidate's present ministry by not telling anyone about this inquiry.

Sincerely,

_____

Chairman or Secretary, Pastor Search Committee

TOOL 20
INTERVIEW QUESTIONS

Good interview questions call for detailed answers rather than a simple yes or no. Do not be afraid to ask hard questions. Use this time to learn as much as you can about the prospect. Following is a comprehensive compilation of questions for a prospective pastor. Select the questions that best fit your needs. Add others that are appropriate for the position. The committee will probably want to receive written responses from the candidate, as well as the verbal responses during the interview, for some questions, such as 1, 13, 43, 44, 45, 59, 60.

Questions for the Candidate

Conversion and Ministry
1. Describe your conversion and your call to ministry.
2. Describe important persons in your life and tell how they influenced you.
3. Describe successes and failures in your ministry.
4. What strengths do you bring to ministry?
5. How have you grown since entering the ministry?
6. In what ways do you need to grow now?
7. How do you allot your time among pastoral ministries?
8. What do you like most about ministry?
9. What do you like least about ministry?
10. Describe your spiritual health and your feelings about spiritual accountability.
11. Describe your personal, private devotional time.
12. Share your plans for personal and professional growth.
13. What doctrines do you think are essential?
14. What are your greatest strengths and your greatest weaknesses?
15. Four major elements of kingdom leadership are leadership, communication, administration, and ministry. Of these areas which do you consider your greatest strength in the ministry and why?
16. How do you measure success in ministry? How do you know when you have done a good or a bad job?
17. Who are your mentors or models in ministry, past or present?
18. Why would you consider moving to another church?
19. How do you classify or describe your preaching style?

Denomination and Community
20. What is your relationship with the denomination?
21. Do you support the Cooperative Program?
22. How active are you in associational work? in state-convention work? In Southern Baptist Convention work? In civic clubs or social organizations in the community?
23. Give us your beliefs about the basic Baptist doctrines as stated in *The Baptist Faith and Message.*
24. How do you relate to other denominations?

Family and Personal Life

25. What do you do for fun and entertainment?
26. Describe your family and tell how each member relates to the others and to the church.
27. Do any of your family members have special needs?
28. How do you encourage spiritual growth in your family?
29. What is your wife's role in your ministry?
30. To what extent is your family involved in your ministry?
31. How would they feel about moving?
32. What do you and your family enjoy doing together?
33. What are your hobbies?
34. Describe your health.
35. Does your family support your calling and vocation?
36. Describe your two closest friends.
37. How do you relate to other ministers?
38. Describe your personal financial situation.
39. What is your philosophy of stewardship and tithing? Do you tithe?
40. Do you have outside business interests? If so, describe them.
41. Describe your exercise program.
42. How many and what books have you read in the past 12 months?

Positions and Policies

43. What is your concept of the Bible?
44. What is your position on missions?
45. What is your conviction on evangelism, and how do you personally practice it?
46. What is your policy on pastoral visitation?
47. What is your policy on pastoral counseling?
48. Do you do personal counseling and, if so, on what level? How extensive is your training in this area?
49. What are your convictions on alcohol and drugs, gambling, pornography, racial prejudice, abortion, homosexuality, and divorce?

Leadership

50. What do you think is the most important thing for you to do during the first year after changing churches?
51. What do you consider, in the order of their importance, your chief duties as pastor?
52. Do you think your best work can be done in a relatively short or a relatively long pastorate?
53. What would the ideal decision-making model look like?
54. What method do you use to accomplish the church's goals and business affairs, such as pastor-led, committee-led, team-led, deacon-led, and so on?
55. What will be your involvement with committees?
56. How do you see the role of deacon in the church?
57. The church allows you to lead revivals and attend conventions and other meetings. How many of these do you normally conduct or attend in a year?
58. What style of public worship and preaching do you prefer?
59. How would you describe an effective worship service?
60. What is your personal belief about the nature and function of the church?

61. Describe your leadership effectiveness.
62. How do you go about making changes in the church?
63. How do you work with church leaders in planning?
64. What role do you see for the laity in the church's decision-making process?
65. How do you keep up-to-date with recent developments in church-related issues?
66. Outline the way you use your time throughout the week.

Staff and Church Relationships

67. What would be your relationship with the church staff?
68. Would you expect to make changes in the current staff?
69. Do you see the staff as being called by the church? Are you willing to work with the present church staff?
70. Do you schedule office hours and days off?
71. Describe your effectiveness in reaching _____.
    (Fill in the blank with a key group of people the church is trying to reach.)
72. Describe how you would communicate with _____.
    (Fill in the blank with a key group of people the church is trying to reach.)
73. How would you rate your interpersonal skills?
74. What is your concept of the role of the laity, both men and women, in the church?
75. What is important to you in handling conflicts between you and a member of the congregation?
76. How do you manage disagreements in your church?
77. How comfortable do you feel in working with all age groups in the church?
78. Discuss your work schedule and the way you divide your time among the responsibilities.

Questions for the Candidate's Wife

1. What influenced your decision to become a Christian?
2. Describe important persons in your life and tell how they influenced you.
3. Describe your personal, private devotional time.
4. Were you aware of your husband's call to ministry before you married?
   If not, explain how you have come to view this call to ministry.
5. How do you relate to the church where your husband is pastor?
6. What is your role in the family?
7. How do you feel about moving?
8. Will you work outside the home?
9. How do you feel about being a minister's wife?
10. What strengths do you bring to your ministry in the church?
11. Describe your family and tell how each member relates to the others and to the church.
12. How do you encourage spiritual growth in your family?
13. What do you and your family enjoy doing together?
14. What are your hobbies?
15. What is your concept of the Bible?
16. What is your position on missions?
17. What is your conviction on evangelism, and how do you personally practice it?
18. What do you appreciate most about your husband?

SERMON EVALUATION

Name of pastor: _____

Date of visit: _____

Name of church: _____

Church address (city and state): _____

Use the following scale to compare this sermon to sermons you are accustomed to hearing in a local church (not on television). Then compute your average at the bottom of the page.

     5 = excellent
     4 = above average
     3 = average
     2 = below average
     1 = seriously deficient

                                             Rating

1. **Introduction.** Captured my attention and interest. Made me want to hear the rest of the sermon.   _____

2. **Scripture.** Used Scripture to make, clarify, and illuminate points. Seemed to be used in context.   _____

3. **Logical continuity.** Points of the sermon logically built on and followed one another.   _____

4. **Clarity.** The purpose and points of the sermon were clear.   _____

5. **Relevance.** The sermon topic was developed in a way that made me see the relevance for myself today.   _____

6. **Humor.** Humor, if used, was appropriate to the setting and points of the sermon.   _____

7. **Self-disclosure.** If the speaker used himself as an illustration, it helped make the sermon more meaningful.   _____

8. **Vocal inflection.** This added appropriate emphasis and interest to the sermon.   _____

9. **Illustrations.** These were used to clarify or deepen the impact of a point, not to prove points.   _____

10. **Interest level.** I would want to hear more sermons from this pastor.   _____

                                           Total _____

Comments: _____

_____ Average (total divided by 10)_____

_____

_____

CREDIT AND LEGAL INFORMATION RELEASE

I hereby authorize _____ Baptist Church,

_____(city and state),

to check my credit and legal history with all appropriate sources. Such information may be obtained for the years

_____ to the present.

Pastor's name: _____

Driver's license number: _____

Social Security number: _____

_____   _____

Pastor's signature   Date

TOOL 23

REQUEST FOR CRIMINAL-RECORDS CHECK AND AUTHORIZATION

I hereby request the _____ Police Department to release any information that pertains to any record of convictions contained in its files or in any criminal file maintained on me, whether local, state, or national. I hereby release the above-mentioned police department from any and all liability resulting from such disclosure.

Signature: _____

Print name: _____

Print all aliases: _____

Date of birth: _____

Place of birth: _____

Social Security number: _____

Today's date: _____

Please send record to: _____

Address: _____

City: _____ State: _____ ZIP: _____

This form is provided for illustrative purposes only. Under no circumstances should a pastor search committee rely on this form without the express, written advice of an independent and qualified attorney, following a full legal analysis of all circumstances.

LETTER TO PROSPECTIVE PASTOR ABOUT QUESTIONNAIRE

Date
Formal heading

Dear _____:

Thank you for your willingness to discuss with our committee the possibility of your coming to serve as the pastor of our church. We are grateful for the opportunity to become better acquainted with your ministry and your family. We certainly believe that this is the direction God wants us to move.

We recognize that we have a responsibility to be honest and open with you in order to build a strong, caring relationship of trust. We also acknowledge a responsibility to meet our church's expectations of us. Therefore, we request that you answer the enclosed questionnaire and return it to us for our files. It includes questions we wish we did not need to ask, but we want to ensure a strong relationship of trust for the future.

If you do not come to serve as our pastor, the questionnaire will be returned to you, and no copies of it will be made. If you become our pastor, the questionnaire will be placed in a closed file and used only to substantiate that the committee followed a thorough process in determining the suitability of the person called to serve as pastor.

Unfortunately, we live in a time of infrequent but occasionally documented abuses by members of the clergy. We also live in a time when churches are not immune to litigation. Please understand that these questions are not meant to insinuate any negative thinking or distrust on our part. We simply need to have this information on file for your protection and for the welfare of the church. If any response is problematic, we can honestly report that the committee discussed it, dealt with it, and made an informed decision to proceed.

You are asked to complete and return the enclosed questionnaire to the chairman of the committee. Thank you for your assistance in this matter.

Sincerely,

_____

Chairman, Pastor Search Committee

PROSPECTIVE-PASTOR QUESTIONNAIRE

Name: _____ Date: _____

1. Have you ever been convicted of any offense other than a traffic violation? ❑ Yes ❑ No
   If yes, explain the circumstances and dispositions. _____
   _____

2. Please list any major traffic violations for which you have been convicted over the past three years.
   _____

3. Have you ever been a party in a civil lawsuit? ❑ Yes ❑ No
   If yes, please explain. _____
   _____

4. Have you ever filed for bankruptcy? ❑ Yes ❑ No
   If yes, please explain. _____
   _____

5. Have you ever been disciplined by any professional, private, or public agency? ❑ Yes ❑ No
   If yes, please explain. _____
   _____

6. Have you ever been dismissed by vote of the congregation from the employment of any church?
   ❑ Yes ❑ No (This question does not imply that you were at fault.)
   If yes, please explain. _____
   _____

7. Have you ever resigned from any church position or employment in the face of charges of misconduct?
   ❑ Yes ❑ No
   If yes, please explain. _____
   _____

8. Have you ever abused or received treatment for alcohol or drugs? ❑ Yes ❑ No
   If yes, please explain. _____
   _____

9. Have you ever been committed, voluntarily or otherwise, to a hospital for psychiatric care?
❏ Yes ❏ No
If yes, please explain. _____
_____

10. Have you ever been formally convicted of spousal or child abuse? ❏ Yes ❏ No
If yes, please explain. _____
_____

11. Have employees, staff, church members, or others with whom you worked ever brought charges of sexual harassment against you before either a church body or any civil governmental agency or court?
❏ Yes ❏ No
If yes, please explain. _____
_____

12. Have you ever initiated any of the following sexual behaviors?

Adultery	❏ Yes	❏ No	Pornography	❏ Yes	❏ No
Homosexuality	❏ Yes	❏ No	Rape	❏ Yes	❏ No
Pedophilia	❏ Yes	❏ No	Incest	❏ Yes	❏ No

If yes for any, please explain. _____
_____

13. Are you a lawful resident or citizen of the United States? ❏ Yes ❏ No

14. Are you currently under continuing medical care for any condition that would affect your ability to carry out a minister's responsibilities? ❏ Yes ❏ No
If yes, please explain. _____
_____

15. How many times have you been married? _____
How many times has your spouse been married? _____

If more than once for either or both, please explain. _____
_____

16. In what states have you held driver's licenses in the past 10 years? _____
_____

_____
Signature

TOOL 26

SERVICE OF INSTALLATION AND COMMITMENT

The Service of Praise

Prelude
Call to Worship
Scripture: "I will tend My flock and I will let them lie down. … I will seek the lost, bring back the strays, bandage the injured, and strengthen the weak" (Ezek. 34:15-16).
Hymn
Invocation
Choir Anthem

The Service of Greeting

Welcome to Guests
Welcome to the Pastor and His Family
- From the community
- From the Baptist association (director of missions)
- From the Baptist state convention

The Service of Commitment

Scripture: 1 Timothy 6:11-21
Solo
The Pastor and the Church in Covenant
- Introduction of pastor to the church and visitors
- Pledges of pastor and people

Leader: (To pastor) Having been called to be the pastor of this church, do you take this people to be your people, this field of labor to be your field, without reservation of mind or heart?

Pastor: I do.

Leader: (To pastor) Do you promise to give yourself faithfully to the ministry, to the Word, and to prayer; to be a good shepherd of this flock of God; to minister to the needs of all alike; to be the friend of all who will permit you; to seek the salvation of souls and the nurture of the saved; to put the services of Christ and His kingdom above all else; if wronged, to forgive as you expect to be forgiven; to seek always to keep yourself mentally alert and physically fit; as much as in you lies, to be at peace with all people; and to lead this church in the ways of Christ as the Holy Spirit gives you wisdom and strength?

Pastor: I do.

Leader: (To congregation) Do you promise to hear attentively the preaching of the Word, to participate reverently in the services of worship, to share with this pastor in the responsibilities of teaching and learning, to assume your proportionate part of the church's benevolent ministries, to receive him into your hearts and homes, to counsel with him about the welfare of the church and the winning of souls, to encourage him in his stand for right, to forgive him when he makes mistakes, and to follow his leadership as he follows Christ?

People: We do.

Leader: Let us together reaffirm our high resolution and devotion to preaching the good tidings of salvation.

People: We consecrate our gifts.

Leader: To teaching Jesus' way of life.

People: We consecrate our time.

Leader: To leading children and youth to the knowledge of the love of Christ.

People: We consecrate our talents.

Leader: To healing broken bodies and soothing troubled minds.

People: We consecrate our service.

Leader: To caring for the helpless and providing relief for all those who look to us for help.

People: We consecrate our strength.

Leader: To evangelizing the community and extending the kingdom of God worldwide.

People: We consecrate our wealth, our efforts, and our lives.

Prayer of Consecration

Hymn of Dedication

Example:

- "Come All Christians, Be Committed," *The Baptist Hymnal* (2008), number 371.

Response of the Pastor

Hymn

Examples:

- "O Master, Let Me Walk with Thee, *The Baptist Hymnal* (2008), number 488.
- "The Church's One Foundation," *The Baptist Hymnal* (2008), number 346.

Benediction

Postlude

TOOL 27

INSTALLATION SERVICE

Organ Prelude

Scriptural Call to Worship .... Member of Pastor Search Committee

Invocation.. Member of Pastor Search Committee

Congregational Hymn .... Congregation

Introduction of New Pastoral Family to Church[1] .... Chairman of Pastor Search Committee

Worship in Music .... Children's or Youth Choir

A Covenant for Ministry Together or Church Covenant .... (Read Responsively)

Scripture .... Member of Pastor Search Committee

Pastoral Prayer .... New Pastor

Congregational Hymn .... Congregation

Offertory Prayer .... Member of Pastor Search Committee

Offertory .... The Doxology

Worship in Music .... Adult Choir

Introduction of Church to New Pastor's Family[2] .... Chairman of Deacons

Signing of Pastor-Church Covenant of Relationship[3] .... Chairman of Pastor Search Committee
and Pastor

Installation Message .... Pastoral Friend or New Pastor

Invitation Hymn .... Congregation

Presentation of Gift[4] .... Chairman of Deacons

Fellowship Hymn and Benediction: "Blest Be the Tie" .... Congregation

---

1. The chairman of the pastor selection committee introduces the new pastor and his family to the church, using biographical information.
2. In introducing the church to the new pastor and family, the deacon chairman briefly recounts highlights from church history.
3. Although "Pastor-Church Covenant of Relationship" (see tool 4) has been signed earlier (see phase 4), this public signing
   will give the covenant greater visibility to the entire congregation.
4. It would be appropriate to present the new pastor a tangible gift to mark the beginning of this new relationship.

PASTOR-CHURCH RELATIONS TEAM

Purpose

The pastor-church relations team serves as a liaison support group between the pastor and the congregation. It is not to serve as an oversight group.

Responsibilities

1. To give relational support to the pastor and his family

2. To serve as a sounding board for the pastor's personal and church concerns

3. To bring the church's concerns to the pastor

4. To be a resource to the pastor in prayer, understanding, and ministry

Procedures

1. The team is composed of six or nine persons who serve on a three-year rotation, with two or three being new appointees each year.

2. The pastor recommends six or nine persons to the nominating committee. The nominating committee considers these and other appropriate persons, from whom the church nominates six or nine. The persons nominated should represent an appropriate diversity of ages, genders, and opinions.

3. The team meets at least quarterly and/or as needed.

4. The pastor and/or the chairman can initiate a called meeting.

5. The team elects a chairman.

Values

1. This team ensures that the pastor has a support group to whom he can turn for counsel and advice.

2. This team provides a communication link between the congregation and the pastor. This point of contact is particularly important for individuals who don't feel comfortable going directly to the pastor.

3. The pastor has a feedback group whom he can consult to check the congregation's perception of his work.

PERFORMANCE REVIEW

The church's personnel committee can use this form in an annual evaluation of the pastor.

Please rank your pastor's performance for the past year in the categories that follow. Your evaluation should reflect his typical performance rather than occasional, isolated performance.

   1 = unacceptable
   2–3 = poor
   4–6 = commendable
   7–8 = outstanding
     9 = consistently superior

Circle one number in each line.

Pastoral Ministry

Communication skills	1	2	3	4	5	6	7	8	9
Listening skills	1	2	3	4	5	6	7	8	9
Counseling skills	1	2	3	4	5	6	7	8	9
Crisis ministry	1	2	3	4	5	6	7	8	9
Hospital visitation	1	2	3	4	5	6	7	8	9
Visitation of shut-ins	1	2	3	4	5	6	7	8	9
Visitation of church members	1	2	3	4	5	6	7	8	9
Grief follow-up ministry	1	2	3	4	5	6	7	8	9
Conduct of funerals	1	2	3	4	5	6	7	8	9
Conduct of weddings	1	2	3	4	5	6	7	8	9

Pulpit/Worship Ministry

Planning of worship services	1	2	3	4	5	6	7	8	9
Planning of prayer meetings	1	2	3	4	5	6	7	8	9
Sermon preparation	1	2	3	4	5	6	7	8	9
Sermon delivery	1	2	3	4	5	6	7	8	9
Sermon variety	1	2	3	4	5	6	7	8	9
Involvement of staff and church members	1	2	3	4	5	6	7	8	9
Teaching skills	1	2	3	4	5	6	7	8	9
Conduct of church ordinances	1	2	3	4	5	6	7	8	9

Church Administration

Leadership of church staff	1	2	3	4	5	6	7	8	9
Leadership of volunteers	1	2	3	4	5	6	7	8	9
Assistance to committees, officers, organizations	1	2	3	4	5	6	7	8	9
Organizational skills	1	2	3	4	5	6	7	8	9

Promotional skills	1	2	3	4	5	6	7	8	9
Timeliness in correspondence	1	2	3	4	5	6	7	8	9
Response to telephone calls, emails	1	2	3	4	5	6	7	8	9
Responsible management of church finances	1	2	3	4	5	6	7	8	9
Delegation skills	1	2	3	4	5	6	7	8	9

Personal Qualities

Grooming/appearance	1	2	3	4	5	6	7	8	9
People skills	1	2	3	4	5	6	7	8	9
Affirmation of others	1	2	3	4	5	6	7	8	9
Balance in life	1	2	3	4	5	6	7	8	9
Physical health	1	2	3	4	5	6	7	8	9
Emotional health	1	2	3	4	5	6	7	8	9
Spiritual health	1	2	3	4	5	6	7	8	9
Family health	1	2	3	4	5	6	7	8	9
Commitment to personal growth	1	2	3	4	5	6	7	8	9
Commitment to professional growth	1	2	3	4	5	6	7	8	9
Punctuality	1	2	3	4	5	6	7	8	9

Community/Denominational Participation

Participation in local Baptist association	1	2	3	4	5	6	7	8	9
Participation in state and national denominational activities	1	2	3	4	5	6	7	8	9
Participation in local clergy association	1	2	3	4	5	6	7	8	9
Image in community	1	2	3	4	5	6	7	8	9
Commitment to local and worldwide missions	1	2	3	4	5	6	7	8	9

Evangelism Leadership

Provision of evangelism training	1	2	3	4	5	6	7	8	9
Commitment to evangelistic visitation	1	2	3	4	5	6	7	8	9
Commitment to evangelistic fervor in the church	1	2	3	4	5	6	7	8	9

Narrative Evaluation

1. What strengths are most evident in the pastor's service and ministry?

_____

_____

_____

_____

2. What areas of the pastor's ministry and service provide the greatest need and opportunity for growth?

_____

_____

_____

_____

3. How did the pastor respond to last year's evaluation?

_____
_____
_____
_____

4. What is the pastor's overall effectiveness and potential in his current role?

_____
_____
_____
_____

5. How effective is the pastor in leading the church to fulfill its purpose and mission?

_____
_____
_____
_____

6. What constructive suggestions do you wish to communicate to the pastor?

_____
_____
_____
_____

This performance review represents a consensus and composite of evaluations completed by the members of the personnel committee.

_____   _____

Signature of chairman, personnel committee   Date

Pastor's written response to the performance review (optional):

_____
_____
_____
_____
_____

_____   _____

Signature of pastor   Date

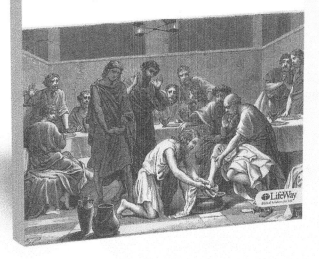

Today's best leadership model is two thousand years old.

How do you train people to do kingdom work?
By following the pattern of Jesus' ministry. This
six-session Bible study, which includes leader helps,
will show you how to apply biblical principles to
develop church members into servant leaders.